CREATE MOTIVATION A
USING **FIVE CRITICAL**

DANCING WITH AN OCTOPUS

How to stop telling and start coaching

Benedict J. Larkey

Harry, Emilia and Joel,
who wondered why questions mattered
and accepted their Dad's obsession.

Now you know why.

ABOUT THE AUTHOR

Ben is one of Australia's leading facilitators and executive coaches.

His experience with and exposure to leaders of large and medium companies through his facilitation of team-building strategy workshops and running corporate training programs have given him an enormous insight into the pressures and challenges leaders face in their roles.

Ben's board appointments, governance experience, capital raising, reporting to shareholders and the successful sale of a business to an ASX200 company have given him personal experience and insights into the requirements of building a successful business. His service with the Australian SAS and high-profile facilitations, including his role as the Prime Minister's Office Facilitator Advisor for the 2020 Summit (2009), provide added perspective and understanding when dealing with high-pressure and challenging environments.

Ben's executive coaching is delivered from a high performance and self awareness perspective. His executive coaching aims for accelerated, meaningful and measurable behaviour and personal satisfaction outcomes.

He has worked in Australia, Asia, the UK and North America. His clients include ANZ, Deloitte, Simplot, Credit Union Australia, St Barbara, Mercer, Westpac, Medibank, Energy Australia, Telstra, Victoria University and Melbourne University.

ACKNOWLEDGEMENTS

This book has been many years in the making, and so many people have influenced me. Thank you to everyone I have had the privilege of working with. To the leaders who trusted me with their teams and to the program participants (the original Octopuses), a sincere and heartfelt thank you for your help over the years. You have been generous and forthright with your responses and feedback. This book has been written with you all in mind and spirit.

A book like this takes enormous amounts of feedback and coaching. Here are some of the special influencers that helped me shape this story.

My first 'dance instructor', Dick Lonergan, Platoon Sergeant, 3 Platoon, A Company, 1 Royal Australian Regiment, a great non-commissioned officer who lifted my performance with great 'pivot' questions and was the master of 'edge' moments. Thank you.

My twin brother, Andrew, who is the most honest person and change agent I know. Thank you for giving me feedback for years to capture what I do and change the way I think.

So many great people have inspired me to be better and clearer in what I do. These are not in order; they all matter: Dan Larkey, Jason McSpeerin, Val Madsen, Alec Bashinsky, Liz McAuliffe, Glenn Jackson, Christine Linden, Tania Motton, Gavin Heathcote, Simone Tilley, Katrina Lewin, Tim Drinkall, Victoria Chow, Mette Schepers, Steve Chugg, Paul Sainsbury, Lauren Pemberton, Michelle Griffin, Jessica Snow, Jill Tulloch, Dominic Eggers, Jeremy Hodgson, Karen Rule, Peter Foggin and Sam Larkey. Special mention to Sue and Jim Larkey, the original dance teachers in my life.

To my many editors, thank you: Sue Larkey, Rosyln Muir, Lisa Rowden, Dennis Verrios, Melanie Smith and Vanessa Fodera. Any mistakes found in the book are down to me, not you. Cristian (at Red Box), your design eye, layout and speed are exceptional and admired.

And to my favourite Octopus, Melanie, for everything.

CONTENTS

READY?

PART A

THE LEADERSHIP CHALLENGE

We cannot teach people anything;
we can only help them discover
it within themselves.

Galileo (1565-1642)

HOW TO CREATE SELF-MOTIVATED PEOPLE

How many challenges would be solved if the person you were working with was self-motivated and capable of solving their own challenges?

Here is the dilemma! To get others to think and do more, you have to tell less.

To get self-motivation, you need the person to be accountable. Accountability means they will do what they are supposed to do. Motivation means that they want to do it. The person needs to recognise the value of the activity and be 'self-motivated' to perform it well.

Self-motivation exists when accountability and motivation happen at the same time. The combination means the 'somebody' will do 'something' because they believe it matters. That 'something' could be anything from how they approach a task, deal with feedback or talk to a customer to how they manage their time or solve their own problems. It would be done with or without supervision and the person would keep improving through doing and reflecting on how they can perform the task better.

What is your experience?

Think of the **best conversations** you have: the ones where what was said mattered, motivated you, made you feel special or respected, that got a relationship back on track or impacted your life. What was so special? One of the two people in that conversation was asking questions and listening to the answers. That person stayed in the 'asking' mode for longer than is typical in the everyday average conversation. That person was coaching.

Think of the **worst conversations** you have experienced: the ones where you felt de-motivated, uninspired or frustrated. One of the people in that conversation, unlikely to be you, was probably in 'telling' mode and therefore not finding out what you felt or thought. That person was telling, not coaching.

The only way to get accountability and motivation at the same time from 'somebody' is coaching them. 'Coaching' means asking questions in a sequence that enables the other person to become clear and for them to make a decision. That decision means ownership to do the 'something' and self-confidence to persist and do it better.

'Dancing with an Octopus' helps a person to re-discover their in motivated self.

By telling less and coaching more in every conversation, you will get accountability and better performance from those you coach.

▶ Think of the coaching conversation as a **dance** (page 28).

▶ Think of your dance partner as a friendly **Octopus** (page 26, 40).

▶ Asking **questions** is the music of the conversation (page 117).

▶ There are **Five Critical Moments**, defined by questions, that enable the dance to achieve both accountability and self-motivation. Each of the five moments are designed to impact the conversation and invoke a specific response from the dance partner. Each moment serves a purpose, which will be shared throughout this book. (page 46)

'A life is made up of a great number of small incidents and a small number of great ones' *Going Solo, by Roald Dahl*

1 Pivot

2 Gap

3 Edge

4 Convertor

5 Able 2.0

HOW THIS BOOK WORKS

Every conversation is a coaching opportunity

Why are we talking about **conversations**? Conversations conducted with the right mindset and skill are opportunities to build relationships. They have the following qualities:

▶ **Frequency**: How many conversations do you have each day? Each of these conversations is an opportunity to impact others. Take the time to consider your approach to each conversation so you can achieve the required impact.

▶ **Environment:** Most meaningful change and development occurs through 1:1 conversation - not in meetings or group settings. Waiting for a meeting to change behaviour or influence performance is a missed opportunity.

▶ **Informal**: A more relaxed and informal setting generates a more candid and open dialogue. Openness is key to understanding what someone is really thinking and wanting. When you first embark on coaching, your meetings will likely be structured and will not feel casual. Persist and practice and soon you will be able to create a more informal environment for your coaching conversations.

Use the overview, guides and self-awareness survey

Throughout this book, you will find overviews, quick guides and self-assessment tools to help you master coaching faster:

▶ The **Overview of Dancing with an Octopus** (pages 46–47, 143) gives a birds-eye view of my approach to coaching.

▶ The **Quick Guide to Applying the Five Critical Moments** (pages 128–129) provides a summary of the Five Critical Moments to coaching - you choose your moment based on your needs.

▶ The **Coaching Self-Awareness Self-Assessment** (page 33). What kind of coach are you? What are your strengths? Where do you need to focus?

You are in control: Read in the order that suits you

Dancing with an Octopus has been designed to be read in a sequence that suits you. Based on the issue facing you or your 'Octopus', just move to the Critical Coaching Moment that will work for you.

Have your person (Octopus) in mind

Don't be a passive reader. For this book to be meaningful and relevant, I encourage you to consider the real issues you or your team are facing as you read. Choose an issue and follow it through.

Develop your own style for each of the moments

Bring your own personality to the examples in the book. They are there to give you a guide to what the critical coaching moments look like.

Do the exercises and make notes as you read

Dancing is an action sport. By doing the exercises, you will soon develop your own personal style and approach to dancing with your Octopus.

▶ Each exercise considers both the skill and mindset needed to be effective. Coaching needs both to succeed.

▶ Write down your thoughts as you participate in the activities. Writing is proven to generate clarity of thought.

Start straight away - Don't wait!

This is not one of those ideas that takes time to implement. It takes only a moment. This means:

▶ Apply one moment in your next conversation. You don't need to apply all of the moments to start getting better results. Every conversation is a chance to dance.

'Don't wait for the perfect moment.
Take the moment and make it perfect.'

Anonymous

WHY ASKING WORKS AND TELLING WON'T

ASKING VERSUS TELLING

Let's make sure we start by understanding the two choices you have to communicate with the people you work and live with. The two choices are:

The 'Asking' approach   or   **The 'Telling' approach**

'Asking' is...	'Telling' is...
A question to understand a different point of view or find out what the other person is thinking.	Giving advice, an opinion or a recommendation or sharing your experience.
A question that creates self-awareness in the other person about what they are doing.	Responding with an instruction or leading question for what the other person should do.
A question to get the other person to clarify what they mean or what they want to do.	Answering a question when you don't understand why it was asked.

The 'asking' approach is coaching.

When people first hear the term 'coaching' or 'coach', they have different reactions. Some people think of a sporting coach from their younger years. That person was dynamic and delivered inspiring messages to motivate and tell the players what to do. Other people have a romantic perspective about coaching. Romantic coaching is the belief that simply getting the other person to reflect will lead to a change of behaviour. Neither of these are the type of coaches or perspectives of coaching I am talking about.

My approach to coaching is question based, challenging and simple to help you recognise that there are critical opportunities or moments in every conversation you have with the people around you which can create the best outcomes for you and for them.

The intention is to give you a memorable and humorous way to think, and to develop new coaching strategies by beginning to ask instead of tell.

WHY ASKING IS BETTER THAN TELLING

Advantages of the 'asking' approach

▶ You have a greater positive impact on other people in a shorter period of time.

▶ You enable others to lift their ownership and accountability to solve their own problems while increasing engagement.

▶ You harness the talent and potential of those around you.

▶ You build the confidence in the person to think for themselves.

▶ You get to find out how the people around you think and approach their day-to-day challenges.

▶ You are setting a collaborative tone as you are seeking their perspective.

▶ You make the other person feel valued and respected because you have sought their views, ideas or opinions.

▶ You reduce the risk of making a wrong decision because you missed or did not get the right information.

▶ You might learn something that you did not know.

▶ You can uncover ideas or tools for success in a future scenario.

▶ You can be far more challenging of behaviour and performance because you are getting them to recognise what they are doing.

▶ Remember! Whoever is asking the questions is leading the conversation.

IMPORTANTLY, all of these advantages accumulate to create the opportunity for you to be inspiring to work or live with!

THE 70% LEARNING FACTOR. A significant advantage of 'asking' is that 70% of learning occurs on the job, but only if the person recognises the opportunity to learn. Asking a person to reflect on what happened during their day gives *them the opportunity to learn.*

Every day there are many experiences and interactions that provide the opportunity to observe and learn. If the person does not recognise that they have learnt something, they will not appreciate that their skills are transferable to solving other challenges.

By asking questions, you are helping the person to reflect and learn. The simple question that triggers this self-awareness is 'What did you learn today?'

As we will explore in the book, one question will not achieve the impact you want. You need to be persistent and follow up your first question with more questions to help the person get clarity.

Example conversation of how persistent asking can work.

TEAM MEMBER   **MANAGER**

I'm glad the day is over.

There is a lot going on. What did you learn today?

I was too busy. I am struggling to keep up with the customer's demands.

It sounds busy. What has caused the demands?

I am not quite sure. We underestimated how much support we would need to get the work done.

So what would you do differently next time?

I did not sufficiently question the quarterly information that we are given.

How would you do that?

I should have asked more challenging questions about time frames. I could then have managed my workload differently.

So what is the key learning you had from the experience?

Ask more time-frame questions. Hey, you were right! There was learning to be taken from the day.

The disadvantages of the 'telling' approach

▶ You are taking on the increased work burden and risk because team decisions and review of the team's work come to you.

▶ You might (but probably not) be wrong, but you have to be the expert.

▶ It's not appropriate for skilled and motivated workers.

▶ It stops the other person from thinking; instead, they are just reacting.

▶ You can create blockages and waste time as you need to tell the person what they need to know.

▶ The person might not listen (you cannot tell an Adult anything*).

▶ You reduce your own creativity and opportunities for improvement because you are using what has worked for you before in your own experience.

▶ Resistance to new ideas will increase due to the lack of consultation and input from other people around you.

▶ Responsibility will lie with you because you 'told' them what to do.

▶ LASTLY, it feels like you are making an impact in the short term, but it is not effective in the medium term.

'Nobody can give you wiser advice than yourself.'

Cicero, Roman Senator (130 BC)

FOR INSIGHT INTO YOURSELF

Take the Self-Assessment Survey

page 33

* You cannot tell an Adult anything until they genuinely recognise they need and want help.

Why people don't respond to being told to change? It is because they have to recognise the need to change for themselves.

Even if the person is asking for your advice or wisdom, do not give it lightly - consider it a last resort. *By delaying your advice, the worst you will be accused of is seeing what they think the solution is first.* You will do less and they will have ownership of their answer because they developed it themselves.

Here is an example conversation of how the 'telling' approach (especially using 'closed' questions) generates resistance and frustration and does not help the other person.

TEAM MEMBER   **MANAGER**

SO WHY DON'T WE STOP TELLING AND START ASKING?

THE #1 OBSTACLE: ARE YOU ADDICTED TO TELLING?

If you are telling, you are working harder than you need to AND wasting the talent of others.

If you were given a choice between telling someone to do something or asking them what they think they should do, which would you choose, Telling or Asking? Most people would say it depends, but what I have seen from practical experience is that most people tell.

Think of your last couple of days at home and at work. How many times have you answered a question about what someone should do? Every one of those questions from a colleague, peer or family member could have been a chance to ask them a question about what they think they should do. Why would you answer the question before asking them what they think first?

Can you stop yourself from telling someone what to do? For most people, the habit is to 'tell' first and 'ask' later. 'Telling' dominates because it seems straightforward and seems efficient. You may have heard these excuses for telling: 'I would ask them but I don't have the time!' 'It is simpler to tell them!' and the classic 'They asked me. I am just answering the question!'

These excuses are an old mindset that will hold you back from the opportunity to find the potential and talent in the other person. Being aware of your 'telling' habit will help you start your new habit of coaching.

Example of Telling versus Asking Conversation

How many conversations do we have where we are not getting the outcome that either person wants, even when we want the best for the other person? A sample conversation between a child and two different adults demonstrates this challenge:

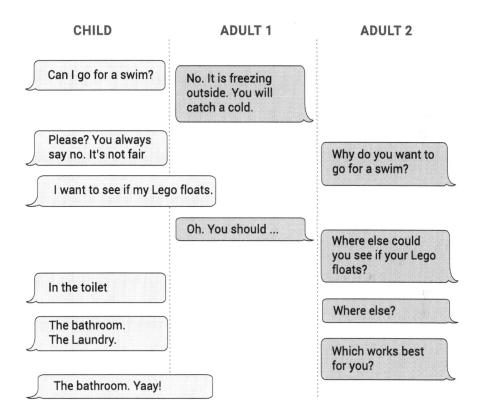

This conversation on the surface seems like just a small misunderstanding, but multiply it by the number of interactions per day, per week, per year and it becomes a relationship crusher. Everyone in the conversation had the best of intentions. The child had not expressed what they were thinking or thought through all the options. Adult 1 was well meaning but had a 'telling' mindset. Adult 2 showed what happens when you ask versus telling.

THE #2 OBSTACLE: BEING A PROBLEM SOLVER.

The biggest challenge to asking is not the other person - it's you!

You want to fix that problem. You want to help them or solve their issue for the them, which means there is no dance - just well-meaning advice (or telling!). It might feel rewarding to you in the short term, but for the other person, this builds dependency on you. They start to see you as the person to solve their problems.

Common excuses for not coaching:

▶ You think it is clearer and more efficient to be direct and tell them.

▶ You have low confidence in the person to do the role.

▶ You do not believe that the person can change.

▶ You don't know any other way.

But what if the other person does not want to dance?

There is a chance that the person does not want to engage with you yet! I say 'yet' because if there is a lack of trust in the relationship between you and the person, they will be reluctant to reveal their thinking when you start asking questions. This situation means the dance will begin slowly. Start the dance and persist with your questions. With the right intention and increasing skill, the person will begin to see that you really want to know what they are thinking. This will build the person's confidence in you, which will allow the conversation to flow.

Example of a Problem-Solving Conversation

How much potential has been missed in the workplace? A sample conversation between a manager and a team member demonstrates this challenge:

TEAM MEMBER   **MANAGER**

In this conversation, you can see that the team member has some thinking to untangle. The Manager does not understand the real issue the team member is grappling with. The Manager answered the questions, gave advice and offered wisdom but did not help the team member explore and expand their thinking. This might have been OK, but it could have been a much more powerful conversation if it had been a dance instead of a 'tell'.

THE CHALLENGE IS TO OVERCOME THESE OBSTACLES AND GET OTHERS TO:

SOLVE THEIR OWN ISSUES

CHANGE THEIR BEHAVIOUR

GET BETTER OUTCOMES

BE INSPIRED!

PART B

THE DANCE AND THE OCTOPUS

Problems are not stop signs,
they are guidelines.

Robert H. Schuller

WHY COACHING IS LIKE DANCING

Coaching is...

The *process and skill* of asking a person what they think.

The quality of the coaching is driven by the *questions* you choose to use.

Those questions become more powerful when they are placed in an *order and sequence* to create a flow.

That flow is the *dance*. The dance is the *coaching* that allows the person to become clearer about their issues and start to see opportunities to do things better.

Dancing develops the *thinking and awareness* that something can be done differently and leads to a *willing commitment* to act.

That *decision* to act means the person owns the outcome of their choice and is invested in what happens next to change behaviour and improve performance.

The coach is *guiding the dance* to improve the person's self-awareness, confidence, willingness and ability to take action.

Now the warning: Every time you 'tell' the person what to do, you stop the dance. You are imposing your thinking onto the person. You are no longer partners.

If you want to inspire others, increase accountability, change behaviour and get better outcomes, then *stop telling and start dancing.*

WHY YOU NEED CRITICAL COACHING MOMENTS IN YOUR DANCE

You will remember moments not a process

Pivot

Gap

Edge

Convertor

Able 2.0

The reason we need to think of *coaching* as moments rather than a process is that moments have more impact. In a moment, you can change the direction of the conversation. The dance can start to move in a new and more productive direction. Each of the moments is so simple and practical that you will remember to use them inside more conversations.

'We don't remember days. We remember moments.' Cesare Pavese

How the Critical Coaching Moments help your dance

▶ **Impact.** Each critical coaching moment is designed to have an impact on the other person, to help them clarify their thinking. The positive impact on another person occurs when you use the targeted question.

▶ **Timing.** Your dance accelerates and in as little as eight minutes can get real performance change. Using the moments reduces the time spent dancing while increasing the impact you are able to have.

▶ **Energy.** The dance partner is energised because you are challenging their thinking about their issues and coming up with options.

▶ **Fun.** Just asking questions is not enough to get change. The critical coaching moments will take the dance in new directions that could be surprising and rewarding.

AND WHY THE OCTOPUS IS YOUR PARTNER

The person is like an Octopus that needs to 'untangle' their thoughts.

Think of the person you are coaching as an Octopus

The Octopus metaphor is chosen to playfully recognise and explore the challenges of working with people with different behaviours and characteristics.

What do you think of when you hear the word Octopus?

Complicated, flexible, tangled, sticky, smart, adaptable, dangerous?

The overwhelming reaction to an Octopus is that 'they are not simple or straight forward!'

Harnessing a person's potential, experience and skill is like trying to wrestle an Octopus. Where do you start? Which issue – or in this case, tentacle – do you grab first?

Your ability to identify and target the tentacle (or issue) will be an important starting place for the coaching you will be doing.

The Octopus has suckers which they used to grip and hold onto objects. A coaching conversation can feel like that. The person being coached may need to 'let go' of old habits or behaviours. Choose one 'tentacle' (issue) and stick with that. As you ask questions, the Octopus can start to express their thinking which in turn helps them to 'untangle' their thoughts and explore options for them to consider.

DANCING WITH AN OCTOPUS MEANS ASKING QUESTIONS

Questions are the skill that makes dancing effective

The questions you choose to ask help develop the thinking and engagement with the Octopus.. Think of the questions as the key to the dance. By asking questions, you start to unravel and recognise what they think and feel.

Questioning is based on the foundation of listening. Listening is demonstrated by your response to what was said. Your responsive questions will give your conversation a sense of flow and movement.

The Power of 3 Plus: The Skill of the Dance

The Power of 3 Plus looks like a questioning technique but is all about listening. The questions you ask must come from the response to your previous question. Each question will follow from the preceding answer. You need to do this at least three times to get past the superficial responses and get to specific, unique and meaningful thinking. This flow of linked questions is how you create the music of the dance.

Asking will become a habit

Asking will become a habit that you use with more and more people. As you appreciate that the Octopus has greater potential than you (or they) realise, then you will start to ask more questions to find out what they are thinking.

FOR MORE INFORMATION

Questioning
Masterclass
page 117

THE DANCING MINDSET

The reality is that a coaching conversation will change direction and have twists and turns as the Octopus clarifies their thinking. That means coaching cannot be rigid and prescriptive. Coaching needs a far more engaging and flexible mindset to be successful.

A dancing mindset creates freedom and impact

There are six mindsets necessary for great dancing (coaching). Imagine what your coaching would look like by going into every conversation with these mindsets:

MINDSET: BE CURIOUS

You want to know what they are thinking and why they are behaving in certain ways.

☐ What are they thinking?

☐ Ask more questions instead of telling.

☐ Look beyond the surface of events.

MINDSET: BE SPECIFIC

If you can help the Octopus to be specific, they will become clear and focused about what they are thinking.

☐ What do they mean?

☐ Ask them to give more details.

☐ Ask them for examples.

MINDSET: BE ALIGNED

You and the Octopus need to be dancing with the same 'tentacle'. By staying aligned on the same issue, you can control the dance and implement the critical moments introduced next to you.

☐ Are you both talking about the same thing?

☐ Accept the complexity of the Octopus.

☐ Help them to prioritise their issues.

MINDSET: BE TIME BOUND

You have targeted time expectations. You both know when the dance is going to finish.

Tip: A skillful dance should take 10–12 minutes.

☐ Are we focused?

☐ Manage the time allocated for dancing.

☐ Maintain momentum in your coaching.

MINDSET: BRING ENERGY

For a dance to work, you will need to bring and create energy. You do this by changing the direction of the dance and moving the conversation faster than the Octopus expects.

☐ Are you both engaged?

☐ Be energised when you see the other person developing.

☐ Is the other person really thinking about their answers?

MINDSET: SEEK MUTUAL VALUE

Both dance partners should get what they need and not just what you want. Don't leave a dance without trying to finding value for both of you.

☐ Are we both getting value?

☐ Work on something that is worthwhile.

☐ Believe that helping this Octopus will positively impact you as well.

EXERCISE 1: DANCING MINDSET CHECK

			IMPORTANT:
What you will need:	Self-awareness, space to think		Every exercise in the book will refer to one of the
How long it will take:	10 min		Dancing Mindsets that will help you to complete
Dancing mindset:	Be Curious		the task.

You've read through the key characteristics that make up the Dancing Mindset: Be Curious, Be Specific, Be Aligned, Bring Energy, Be Time Bound, Bring Mutual Value. Now take a moment to decide which of these you already consider strengths and which are the mindsets that you need to keep developing.

Make a note of them here, and refer back to them as you work through the book.

DANCING MINDSET	ALREADY DANCING...	A BIT OF DANCING PRACTICE NEEDED...
Be Curious		
Be Specific		
Be Aligned		
Bring Energy		
Be Time Bound		
Seek Mutual Value		

APPLY THESE MINDSETS TO IMPROVE YOUR CONVERSATIONS AND OUTCOMES.

GREAT QUOTES ABOUT QUESTIONING (AND DANCING)

'He or she that asks a question is a fool for five minutes; he or she who does not remains a fool forever.'

Chinese Proverb

'The power to question is the basis of all human progress.'

Indira Gandhi

'Good Leaders ask great questions that inspire others to dream more, think more, learn more, do more, and become more.'

John C. Maxwell

'We dance for laughter, we dance for tears, we dance for madness, we dance for fears, we dance for hopes, we dance for screams, we are the dancers, we create the dreams.'

Albert Einstein

LET'S FIND OUT HOW YOU ARE DANCING NOW

SELF - ASSESSMENT

ATTITUDE, SKILLS AND IMPACT OF COACHING

EXERCISE 2: SELF-ASSESS: HOW I COACH NOW

What you will need: Pen,   Quiet space

How long it will take: 10 min

Dancing mindset: Be Curious

▶ Intent: Learn to notice what reaction you are getting from others and start to identify what you can work on to improve your coaching.

Section 1: My Mindset About Coaching

Section 2: Getting Ownership from Others

Section 3: My Impact on Others

Section 4: My Coaching Skills

▶ Review and rate the behaviours and challenges you encounter when working with others on the next pages as follows:

This never happens   1

This rarely happens   2

This sometimes happens   3

This happens occasionally   4

This happens all the time   5

▶ For each section, add the scores to create a total and compare that total against the guide on pages 36 and 37.

▶ Select one behaviour from each section that you think you would find the most beneficial to develop as you read the book.

▶ Advanced challenge: Get someone else to complete the questionnaire about you from their perspective.

COACHING ASSESSMENT

SECTION 1: My Mindset About Coaching

	1	2	3	4	5
I find out the reason for something happening	☐	☐	☐	☐	☐
I am more interested in what they think than in my ideas	☐	☐	☐	☐	☐
I ask them to describe their thinking in detail	☐	☐	☐	☐	☐
I find out what they mean and not just what they say	☐	☐	☐	☐	☐
I am able to stay on track when faced with complexity	☐	☐	☐	☐	☐
I am energised when I see the other person grow	☐	☐	☐	☐	☐
I hold back on giving my opinion to others	☐	☐	☐	☐	☐
I get value from being a coach	☐	☐	☐	☐	☐
TOTAL					

SECTION 2: Getting Ownership From Others

	1	2	3	4	5
People keep coming to me to solve their problems	☐	☐	☐	☐	☐
Decisions are passed to me rather made at the right level	☐	☐	☐	☐	☐
Others are holding back on their opinions from me	☐	☐	☐	☐	☐
I invest time in coaching, but nothing really changes	☐	☐	☐	☐	☐
Behaviours in others don't change after feedback	☐	☐	☐	☐	☐
Inconsistent performance on certain tasks	☐	☐	☐	☐	☐
People avoid taking responsibility for their actions	☐	☐	☐	☐	☐
I ask lots of questions but still don't get what I want out of the conversation	☐	☐	☐	☐	☐
TOTAL					

SECTION 3: My Impact on Others

	Never 1	Rarely 2	Sometimes 3	Occasionally 4	All the time 5
Individual's confidence grows from working with me	☐	☐	☐	☐	☐
Individuals volunteer and show initiative	☐	☐	☐	☐	☐
Individuals learn quickly and share their knowledge	☐	☐	☐	☐	☐
Individuals improve from making mistakes	☐	☐	☐	☐	☐
I am told by others that I am inspiring	☐	☐	☐	☐	☐
People want to work with me	☐	☐	☐	☐	☐
I am seen as good at developing the talents of others	☐	☐	☐	☐	☐

TOTAL

SECTION 4: My Coaching Skills

	1	2	3	4	5
I have a coaching method that I follow	☐	☐	☐	☐	☐
I consciously 'ask' versus 'tell' with others	☐	☐	☐	☐	☐
I ask questions that get to the important issues	☐	☐	☐	☐	☐
My coaching finishes within the expected time frame	☐	☐	☐	☐	☐

TOTAL

SUMMARY SCORE   TOTALS

Section 1: My Mindset About Coaching

Section 2: Getting Ownership From Others

Section 3: My Impact on Others

Section 4: My Coaching Skills

How to interpret the self-assessment results

SECTION 1: My Mindset About Coaching

Score	Meaning
>30	You have a high level of flexibility and adaptability when you are working with others. You have a good coaching mindset and can see personal benefit in coaching.
20-29	You are in the difficult zone of having some effective attitudes. However, you may be lacking some consistency. You need to develop targeted areas of your mindset and approach to coaching.
<19	Your mindset is likely affecting your coaching. This attitude to coaching will be important to develop in order for you to adopt new skills. See pages 28 and 29 for further help.

SECTION 2: Getting Ownership From Others

Score	Meaning
>25	You are not getting the best from the people around you. This indicates that although you are working hard, you are not taking responsibility for what they are doing. You have the opportunity to start a new dancing approach.
16-25	You have some of the right behaviours and skills that you need to get more from others. However, people have become dependent on you. You need to build a more robust approach to support what you are doing. Check out the Quick Guide on pages 126 and 127.
<15	You are getting good results from the people around you. You are implementing good coaching behaviours. The key is to understand why you are getting those good results and see what you can do to develop further.

SECTION 3: My Impact on Others

Score	Meaning
>25	You have a positive impact on the people around you. This shows that you have been able to get people to change their performance and reach their potential.
16-25	You have components of effective coaching behaviour but are missing consistency. To change these results, embrace everyday conversations and use the moments to become a better coach.
<15	You are missing the benefits of coaching others. The benefit of coaching comes through in this assessment. These are behavioural indicators that show that people around you are not seeing you as a coach. You should adopt new coaching skills into your conversations.

SECTION 4: My Coaching Skills

Score	Meaning
>15	You have a good coaching skill base. The challenge is to keep a written account. Challenge yourself by checking out the Able 2.0 moment on page 103.
6-14	You are missing some critical skills. Your questioning technique will improve by using the Rule of 3 Plus. Check out page 115. To evaluate your conversation time allocation, check out pages 128 and 129.
<5	You have an intuitive approach to coaching. You will benefit from the simple, practical approach of this coaching method. Check out the overview of the coaching method on pages 46 and 47.

Check out pages 126 and 127 for strategies, moments and skills to achieve positive behaviours and change.

EXERCISE 3: REFLECTION – MY AREAS TO DEVELOP

What you will need: Completed self-assessment, Quiet space for reflection

How long it will take: 10 min

Dancing mindset: Be Curious

After completing the survey, reflect on what areas you most want to develop.

WHAT IS THE MOST IMPORTANT NEW IDEA FOR YOU?

WHAT ARE THE SPECIFIC AREAS YOU WANT TO DEVELOP?

▶ From each section, select one behaviour you want to develop as you read the book.

▶ Convert the problem statements into the positive outcomes that you are looking for.

FROM	>	TO
Example:.		
People keep coming to me to solve problems they can solve themselves.	>	*Individuals come to me with options and alternatives.*
1.	>	
2.	>	
3.	>	
4.	>	

WHO IS YOUR OCTOPUS?

FROM HERE ON IN THIS BOOK, THE
PERSON BEING COACHED IS CALLED

THE **OCTOPUS**

ET YOUR OCTOPUS

ngle thinking to get action

from the perspective that the Octopus you are coaching can untangle
selves — your role is to help them. This sounds simple enough, but
challenge is that the Octopus sometimes cannot see their potential or
ay ahead. Here are some common reasons the Octopus needs to dance
with you:

Octopus has lost *confidence* in their ability

Octopus is *delaying*
making a decision

Octopus is *struggling*
to solve an issue

Octopus is *blaming* others for
what they should have done

Octopus has *something*
on their mind

Octopus is doing well but
can *be doing better*

Octopus has *lost* focus on
what they want to achieve

Octopus is *avoiding* an issue
that they need to deal with

Octopus is *defensive* about
something they are doing

To untangle their thinking and help them solve their
own problems, you will need to identify which tentacle
(issue) to focus on.

EXERCISE 4: OCTOPUS TENTACLE IDENTIFICATION

What you will need:	Self-awareness, space to think.	Intent: To practice tentacle issue identification before you speak to the Octopus.
How long it will take:	10 min	
Dancing mindset:	Be Specific	

▶ *Identify the key people* with whom you want to have a better relationship or whose performance you'd like to help enhance.. Write their name in the circle.

▶ *Identify the 'tentacles or issues* you have observed. Use the list on the previous page to help your thinking.

▶ *Remember.* This is only your perspective. Issues will become clearer as you find out more information from the Octopus.

Make a note of the issues here and refer back to them as you work through the book. Tick off the box when you have applied the 'Dancing with an Octopus' method to them in the application exercises.

Who is an Octopus that you can develop?	List of key tentacles that you need to dance with?	Tick when completed

EXAMPLE

Sarah

1. *Has lost her confidence*
2. *Is struggling with her workload*
3. *Has unrealised potential*

1.

2.

3.

EXERCISE 4: OCTOPUS TENTACLE IDENTIFICATION

Who is an Octopus that you can develop?

List of key tentacles that you need to dance with?

Tick when completed

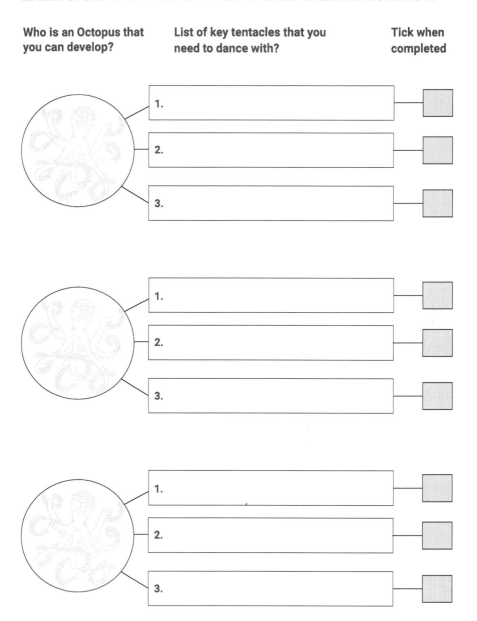

PUT ON YOUR DANCING
SHOES, TAKE YOUR
OCTOPUS BY A TENTACLE,
AND LET'S START
DANCING

NOTES PAGE

PART C

THE FIVE CRITICAL COACHING MOMENTS

Sometimes you will never
know the value of a moment
until it becomes a memory.

Dr Seuss

DANCING WITH THE FIVE CRITICAL COACHING MOMENTS™

In every conversation, there are five critical moments that will give you the maximum impact on the Octopus's thinking and performance. Asking one of these targeted, critical questions at the right moment changes the direction of the dance and helps the Octopus to create their own solution.

1. The Pivot Moment

The moment when you change the focus of the conversation to the Person instead of the Problem.

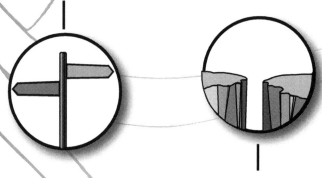

2. The Gap Moment

The moment when they identify and articulate the gap between 'What is happening' (reality) and 'What is wanted' (goal).

The moments are so simple and powerful, that you can *use all or a combination* of them in every conversation you have.

Power of 3 Plus is the skill that works with the critical coaching moments to generate real thinking and better outcomes. This skill makes listening tangible rather than an attitude. It is what makes the coaching conversation feel like a dance.

5. Able 2.0 Moment

The moment when you get them to practice and demonstrate that they are able to do what they need to do next.

3. The Edge Moment

The moment when you critically challenge their solution against reality, the goal or the gap between the two.

4. The Convertor Moment

The moment you can stay as coach by converting your concerns and experience into questions to accelerate the conversation.

TIME ALLOCATION

The Five Critical Coaching Moments can help you move through your dance effectively and efficiently. You are the leader in the dance, and therefore you can choose WHEN to use the moments.

Allocate a time frame for the dance

Set the time with your Octopus. Shorter, more effective conversations are part of the new way of thinking about the way you interact with the Octopus. You can schedule another meeting if you need more time.

Guidelines for how long your dance should be

The Three Types of Dances	Ideal Duration
The Octopus asks you a question. See what they think first. Choose just one or two critical moments, e.g. Pivot or Gap.	2–3 minutes
Simple issue. The Octopus is open to questions but lacks clarity or confidence. Try to identify and focus on a single 'tentacle' issue. In this dance, you may use all the moments.	8–10 minutes
Complex issue. The Octopus is closed, defensive or has many relating issues. The advantage of limiting a complex dance to a specific time is that you can 'push' the conversation along with the Octopus. To see what the Octopus's reaction might be, go to the Edge moment or the Able 2.0 moment.	18–20 minutes

Dancing Mindset required

Be Time Bound: Move the dance forward to meet the time expectations.

Be Aligned: Get clarity on the tentacle you are targeting.

TIMING GUIDE

Here is the time allocation guide to help you determine when each of the five critical moments should be used and how long they should take.

	During Dance	How much time	Reason
Pivot	First > 2 min	1–2 min	Pivot within the first 2 min of the conversation. The longer you are talking about the problem, the more likely you are to become a problem solver.
Gap	< 1/2 way	1–2 min	Create the Gap moment before the halfway mark in the time allocated to the dance. This gives you time to make sure there is a clear outcome and motivation to act.
Edge	By 1/2 way	3–4 min	Get to what they can do differently by he halfway mark in the dance. This will allow you time to use the Edge moment to get more ideas and more commitment to their solutions.
Convertor	As required	2–3 min	The Converter moment is used by you to accelerate the dance. Use the Convertor moment when you want to progress the thinking of the Octopus or when you want to give advice.
Able 2.0	Last 2 min	2–3 min	The Able 2.0 moment ensures that the Octopus will take the first step. This moment happens in the last 2-3 minutes. Make it realistic to have maximum impact.

EXAMPLE OF DANCING USING
THE FIVE CRITICAL COACHING MOMENTS™

This coaching conversation has been edited and slightly condensed to show what Dancing using the Five Critical Moments looks like. [The coach is a peer of the Octopus.]

COACH

OCTOPUS

What is a challenge that you are dealing with?

I want my team to look for opportunities to improve their performance.

Start the Dance.

What is the main issue you want to change?

They do not interact enough with each other. Our team meetings are not valuable or that helpful.

What have you tried so far to resolve this?

I have asked them to look at how they can help each other deal with challenges they are facing.

What happened next?

It made the situation worse.

Worse in what way?

MOMENT #1: The Pivot. From the problem to the person.

What do you think you are missing then?

Now they don't bring anything that is difficult to discuss to the team meetings.

Me?

Yes.

I guess I haven't addressed the dynamic or the lack of trust in the group.

COACH   **OCTOPUS**

What is the impact of you not addressing the trust issue?

It means that I have not set the right expectations for the group. In fact, I have done the opposite.

In what way?

On reflection, I like to create healthy competition, but I can see that is not working.

MOMENT #2: The Gap. The gap between what happened and what they want.

What is the behaviour you want them to show in the team meeting? Be specific.

I want them to bring their problems and get the other team members to see how they can help.

That is different to what you are getting now. What can you do to enable this?

I need to explain what I want and ask them to be more open with each other.

MOMENT #3: The Edge. Challenge the option or solution.

'Telling them' sounds very similar to what you have already done. What else could you try?

(Pause) I can't think of what else to do.

MOMENT #4: The Convertor. Convert concerns to questions.

What are your options other than telling them?

Ask the team what they think?

What would you ask them?

What they think we need to do differently?

How similar is that question to what you have tried before?

I have not talked about 'how' we are working. It has been more about 'what' we are doing.

COACH

OCTOPUS

So what will you say to introduce the question in the team meeting?

Oh... that's a good question. I need to think that through.

 MOMENT #5: Able 2.0: They take the first step with you.

Take a moment, then try it out with me.

Ok. Let me think about this. [Pauses] This is harder than I thought.

Take your time. By practicing it with me, we can get it right.

OK, here goes. 'Team, I want to start a conversation about how we work together instead of what we do. I am going to ask each of you to think about what *I need to change* to help you work better together.

What did you think of the practice?

That was better. I liked how I made it about me changing to give them a better environment where it's safer to contribute.

When will you be able to have this meeting?

My next meeting is next week. I will let you know what happens.

That would be great. I would love to hear what you learn from doing it this way.

ARE YOU READY TO DANCE WITH AN OCTOPUS?

The Octopus has tentacles (issues) that need to be untangled

Beware the addiction of telling

Coaching means asking questions

Listening means your questions build on what the other person has said

Having a Dancing Mindset means you need to:

- *Be Curious - What are they thinking?*
- *Be Specific - What do they mean?*
- *Be Aligned - Are we talking about the same thing?*
- *Bring Energy - Are we engaged?*
- *Be Time Bound - Are we focused?*
- *Seek Mutual Value - Are we both getting value?*

LANGUAGE AND DEFINITIONS

Coaching is the mindset and skills used to enable clarity for another person to commit to a choice of action.

Dancing means coaching.

Dancing is a metaphor for the mindset that guides the interaction between the coach and the coachee.

Octopus refers to the coachee, the person being coached.

Tentacle is the issue that you are focusing on in your dance with the Octopus.

NOTES PAGE

MOMENT 1

THE PIVOT

'You cannot coach a problem, you can only coach a person'

Ben Larkey

You have started the dance with a question. Keep asking questions based on what your Octopus says to keep the dance going. You are now ready to introduce the first critical moment – the Pivot!

A pivot is a central point around which something turns.

The Pivot moment is the question that you, as the coach, choose to ask in the conversation to create self-awareness in the Octopus regarding their role in solving their challenge.

WHY THE PIVOT IS CRITICAL

Coach the person not the problem

The Octopus has an issue. That issue will be an opportunity, dilemma, uncertainty or problem that they need to have clarity on in order to act. If you are asking questions about that issue, you are focusing on the problem and not the Octopus's approach to the problem. You want the Octopus to start focusing on what they are doing in relation to the issue. Your questions now switch to what your Octopus dance partner is thinking. This change of focus to the person is where you lift the conversation from being about 'what' they are doing to 'how' they are doing it. The 'how' of their working, behaving or thinking is far more impactful and repeatable in other situations.

Set the new direction for the Dance

When you Pivot, you change the tempo of the dance and set a new direction. The conversation shifts from discussing the issue to exploring what the person thinks about the issue. The dance will now become about the Octopus.

The Octopus may feel this shift in focus and will reflect it in the language they use. The Octopus starts using words such as 'I' or 'Me' rather than 'they' or 'you'. A sense of ownership is achieved.

The Octopus needs to own their role in solving the issue

The Octopus will know more about the issue they are facing than you will because they are involved in it. Even if you think you have experienced a similar situation, you cannot solve their problem. The Octopus needs to recognise that and take ownership of their problem in order to move forward in finding a solution.

KEY ELEMENTS OF THE PIVOT

The earlier you pivot, the better!

A risk to be aware of is the amount of time you allocate to understanding the problem versus focusing on the person. It is an easy mistake to fall into because often the conversation begins with a problem or request for help. The longer you ask about the problem, the more you will fall into the role of solution giver rather than coach. It breeds dependency on you, removes ownership and does not enable development. The Octopus is the person who must deal with the problem. Therefore, focus on what they are thinking instead of on the problem itself.

Understand just enough about the problem or issue for the Octopus to feel you have the context. Unless you direct your focus to the Octopus, you will become trapped on the problem. You change this by asking the Pivot questions before you get too bogged down in the details of the problem

What is best practice?

After listening to hundreds of coaching conversations, I recommend Pivoting **within two minutes of starting to dance.** The Octopus sometimes wants to give you more detail. Use your own judgment. Pivot as soon as you can.

Multiple problems? Pick the main one

Octopus's will often raise multiple issues as you are dancing. You, as the coach, want to get the Octopus to choose the issue that is most important first. A way to get that mutual clarity is to ask the Octopus to summarise what they think the main issue is. The Octopus may get wrapped up in their own tentacles. Even if all the issues relate to each other, which is likely, keep them separate by dancing with one issue at a time.

How to build a pivot moment

The Pivot moment is a question which asks the Octopus about what they are thinking. When developing your own Pivot questions, they should contain some key words or sentences:

▶ Use 'You': this puts the focus on them

▶ Use 'think': this makes them reflect on the approach they are taking

▶ Reference the Octopus's experience: 'In your experience...' or 'You have seen this before...'

▶ Ask about why it's important to solve this issue: 'What is the impact...'

The problem: What they did

Examples of Problem questions:

What happened?

What caused the problem?

What did you do next?

Why did you do that?

What have you done to fix this?

What could you do about this?

> 'Change the way you look at things
> and the things you look at change.'

Wayne W. Dyer

PIVOT MOMENT QUESTIONS

The person: How they think

Examples of Pivot questions:

What have you tried so far?

What do you believe is the key factor in this issue?

What are you thinking about the issue?

How have you reacted to this issue?

What impact did this have?

How important is a solution to you?

Reactions to the Pivot

The Pivot is a powerful moment in coaching.

The Pivot will come as a surprise if you normally solve the Octopus's problems for them or give advice. The Pivot signals that the dance is changing direction and becoming about 'how' the Octopus is thinking. This question slows down the dance because you are shifting their focus and they have to think about their role in the issue. Watch for the slowing down in responses from the Octopus as an indicator that the Pivot is working.

CASE STUDY: MIKE

Mike approaches his manager with an issue that he is dealing with.

Dancing with Mike. Moment 1

You can follow the coaching conversation with Mike over the next four instalments. The next installment is page 72.

COACH

MIKE

> I have a problem I need your help with.

> Sure, what is the issue?

> I am finding it tough to work with Sam. He is defensive and is not responding to my requests.

> What requests have you made?

> Nothing that you wouldn't expect. Mainly to do with forecast numbers for his project.

 MOMENT 1: The Pivot from the problem to the person.

> That is an important request. What have you done so far to address the issue?

> I have told him how important the forecast numbers are and how not having them affects my team.

 MOMENT 1: Repeat the Pivot question if the Octopus does not shift focus.

> You are still talking about the work request. What have you tried to do so far to address his lack of response?

> Oh well, I have not talked about that with him yet. He gets defensive if I try raising anything with him.

> So what do you believe is causing his defensive behaviour when working with you?

> Well, I am not sure, but I think he is feeling under resourced and I am coming in to ask for more.

> So you are not sure?

> You're right. I have not tried to find out what is causing his defensiveness.

Dance continues

What if the Octopus will not Pivot?

The Octopus may put up some barriers to your switching the dance from the problem to them. Here are possible reactions you may experience:

▶ Avoidance: 'It's not my issue. It's theirs.'

▶ Defensive: 'I have done everything I can.'

▶ Open but unaware: 'I don't understand why you are asking me that..'

▶ Helpless: 'I don't know.'

▶ Dependent: 'I am not sure. What do you think?'

Response to the Reactions

Recognise that you have effectively Pivoted – well done!

The first reaction can sometimes be a habit from the Octopus. After a good Pivot, the Octopus might need time to process their answer; pause and find out why they have reacted by asking for more detail.

Be prepared to ask the Pivot question *again* once you feel the Octopus has expressed their concerns. See below for some examples of responses.

EXAMPLES OF FOLLOW-UP QUESTIONS TO A PIVOT MOMENT REACTION

'It not my issue. It's theirs.'	>	'What makes you say that?'
'I have done everything I can.'	>	'What have you done?'
'I don't know.'	>	'What are you missing?'
'What do you think?'	>	'I want to hear your view first.'

CASE STUDY: SARAH

The Coach has identified that Sarah has not been contributing in recent team meetings.

Dancing with Sarah. Moment 1

You can follow the coaching conversation with Sarah over the next four instalments. The next installment is page 74.

COACH

SARAH

Sarah, in our last meeting, you were not your usual self. What's on your mind?

I am really tired. My team seem to be putting in the hours, but we seem to be behind and always rushing.

What requests have you made?

We are not delivering on our plans and I am frustrated.

What do you mean frustrated?

We're missing our milestones, yet I am clear in my expectations of when things are due.

MOMENT 1: The Pivot from the problem to the person.

Let's get more specific. What have you done so far?

Well, for example, Harry, one of my experienced people, should be contributing more than he is.

What is the concern about Harry's performance?

He has missed key deadlines with his work.

So what did you do when he missed the deadline?

Applying the Power of 3 Plus here helps to clarify what has really been done.

What did you do to find out the cause of the *change* in performance?

I tried to help him get back on track.

I didn't talk directly about that.

What happens by not directly talking about it?

Harry doesn't know how his performance is affecting me or the team, and I don't really know why he has changed his behaviour.

Dance continues

EXERCISE 5: CREATE YOUR OWN PIVOT QUESTIONS

What you will need:	Pen, Octopus from Exercise 1
How long it will take:	5 min
Dancing mindset:	Be Curious, Be Specific, Be Aligned

▶ Write out the Pivot questions that you can apply in your conversations with an Octopus. Make the questions feel natural to your personal style. By writing them down, you will gain clarity and be able to recall them when you need them.

▶ Tip: Avoid closed questions.

WRITE YOUR OWN PIVOT QUESTIONS

Remember: Once you ask this Pivot question, you need to ask follow-up questions. We call this the Power of 3 Plus (covered on pages 115 – 119).

Q. What if the Octopus does not believe they can solve their issue on their own?

A. You are not asking them to solve it here (that comes later). You are getting them to say what they think about it. This is an Octopus moment. Acknowledge what they have said but stay with what 'they' think.

Q. What if I can solve the issue quickly by telling them the answer?

A. WARNING. In the short term, it might seem efficient to tell the Octopus the answer, but your answer will not create ownership nor will it inspire the Octopus to try new things.

Q. How do I know if the Pivot has worked or not?

A. The language of the Octopus will change. They will start to say 'I' or 'me' rather than 'them' or 'us'. Another indication is the conversation starts to slow and become more reflective. The person is having to think more as they answer. These are good signs that you are listening and responding to what they are saying.

SUMMARY – WHEN TO USE THE PIVOT MOMENT

When the Octopus...

Is blaming others.

Is focused on the task but not on their own approach.

Needs self-awareness about the impact of their actions.

Is capable of solving the problem but not acting on that capability.

Has experienced this issue before.

DANCING MINDSET REQUIRED

Be Curious: What do they think about the issue?

Be Specific: What is the issue that is most important?

Write down where you can use the Pivot moment

NOTES PAGE

MOMENT 2

THE GAP

'Performance and behaviour can only start to change when the gap between what you are doing and what is possible is clear'

Ben Larkey

The Gap is the reason and motivation to change. Identify and articulate the Gap between 'What is happening?' (Reality) and 'What is wanted?' (Goal) to create the awareness that something needs to change.

Definition of Gap: A space or interval; a break in continuity: A difference, especially an undesirable one, between two situations.

IMPORTANT THINGS TO KNOW ABOUT THE GAP

The Octopus focuses on what they want

The Gap moment question takes the dance to a new level. Instead of focusing on what the Octopus has done, you are asking the Octopus to suspend their current reality and think about what they want to achieve. It lifts the Octopus's thinking outside of what they are currently doing and looks into the future. Thinking through to the desired outcome is a way of helping the Octopus to create a compelling reason as to why the issue is important and worth resolving.

Motivation to act or change needs a reason

The goal question is about getting the Octopus to think about what they want or need, transitioning the Octopus to a new mode of thinking and challenging them to explore options with you. By identifying the Gap, discussion can turn to creating solutions to close the gap and reach the goal.

Urgency to act is increased

The dance needs to have purpose and meaning for the partnership to work. Without a gap or or a goal, the partnership is not clear on what it is trying to change. The coach-led partner needs to understand the Gap to increase the importance of solving the issues being talked about.

KEY ELEMENTS OF THE GAP

The goal needs to be clear and specific

The dance now gains momentum. You want the Octopus to start to look for outcomes that they want to achieve. They should be challenged to be specific about the outcome they want by asking questions based on the response the Octopus is giving you. Keep getting the Octopus to express the outcome clearly. Watch that they express the goal in terms of what they want to achieve, not what the other person should do. If they do, use another Pivot moment.

Place a value on closing the Gap

Ask the Octopus to quantify their goal by placing a financial or an emotional value on it to help crystallize the benefit of taking action. This process helps them to resolve their issues in terms of cost versus benefit they will get. If there is little or no value in achieving the goal or closing the gap, then ask why this is an issue. This can lead to a breakthrough in the dance. (Sample questions are on the next page.)

Close the Gap in small steps if necessary

If what the Octopus wants to achieve and where they are at the moment seems too different, then help them focus on the small goals they can establish. The Octopus may struggle to even think of possible solutions because it is so different to what they are currently doing. It is important that you recognise this but persist in getting them to work through the possibilities. Smaller goals provide motivation and can help the Octopus start acting.

Come back to the Gap if the dance starts to slow down

Later in the dance, when you are asking questions about what the Octopus is going to do differently and they hesitate, go back to the Gap. Remind the Octopus of what they said regarding the value of closing the gap. You are helping connect what they said earlier in the dance with the need for them to change what they are doing. The Dancing Mindset means you can always go back and clarify different answers that you have received previously.

How to build a Gap moment

Some suggested techniques for developing Gap questions:

▶ Use 'goal' or 'outcome' words. This moves the Octopus away from the current issues to focus on the end state they are hoping to achieve.

▶ Use 'difference' or 'gap' words. This. makes the Octopus compare and contrast before they move into solution mode.

The Goal questions

Examples of Goal questions:

What does the ideal outcome look like?

What is the one thing that matters most?

What would the new behaviour look like?

If you solve this, what would you see?

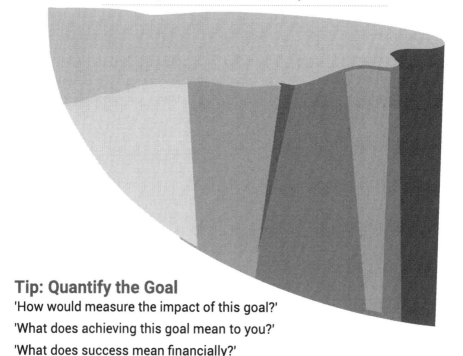

Tip: Quantify the Goal

'How would measure the impact of this goal?'

'What does achieving this goal mean to you?'

'What does success mean financially?'

'Setting goals is the first step in turning the invisible into the visible.'

Anthony Robbins

The Gap questions

Examples of Gap questions:

What is the difference between what you want and what you have said?

How big is the gap you want to close?

What is different about your new goal?

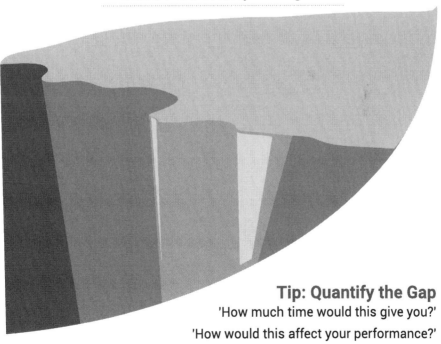

Tip: Quantify the Gap
'How much time would this give you?'
'How would this affect your performance?'
'What is the tangible benefit to you by closing this gap?'

Case Study Continues

Previous: Page 60

Next: Page 84

Dancing with Mike. Moment 2

Update: Mike is now aware that he does not know what is causing the issue with his peer.

COACH   **MIKE**

A goal question to start to identify the gap:

Before we start looking at options, what is the ideal outcome you want with Sam?

> I want us to be able to discuss our priorities together without it getting emotional.

What else?

> It is also very important to get a time-line for how we work to avoid further late requests.

 MOMENT 2: The Gap between what is happening and what they want.

What difference would this make compared to what you have right now?

> It would be a much better way to work. We could then start to meet our agreed targets.

How much would it improve those targets?

> Right now we are 7% behind where we should be. Getting this outcome would help reduce that by at least half.

Any other measures?

> Yes! Stress would be reduced.

Dance continues

Reactions to the Goal and the Gap

WATCH: Usually, the Octopus does not expect Goal and Gap questions. They expect you to go to 'tell' mode! Resist the temptation to go into solution mode.

Here are some of the reactions you may get from the Gap moment question.

▶ It's obvious: I want the opposite. Why are you asking?

▶ Surprise: I had not thought about what I wanted (but I know what I don't want).

▶ Struggle: I cannot express what I want (yet).

▶ Respect: You are asking me what I think. That is an important question for me to reflect on to answer.

EXAMPLES OF HOW TO ASK A FOLLOW-UP QUESTION

'I don't know what I want.'	>	'What would be a first step?'
'It is too hard to express!'	>	'Take your time. It matters.'
'I want the opposite.'	>	'What would that look like then?'
'What do you think?'	>	'I want to hear your view first?'

Case Study Continues

Previous: Page 62

Next: Page 86

Dancing with Sarah. Moment 2

Update: Sarah recognises she has not been effective at holding people to account. The specific example of this is with an experienced team member, Harry.

COACH

SARAH

> What would it look like if you were able to hold Harry and team members to account?

> Harry and the team would do what they say they are going to do.

> What specifically would that look like?

> Less re-work and less delay

> What else would happen if this worked?

> I could find time to work on the more important long-term planning we need to do.

> What amount of time would you be saving by doing less re-work?

> At least 3 hours a week. Maybe more.

MOMENT #2: The Gap

> So what is the gap you need to close with Harry's behaviour?

> I need to get Harry back to his old self and positively influencing the team.

> What would that look like?

 Applying the Power of 3 Plus helps to clarify the Gap and Goal.

> Harry would come to me in advance with issues and concerns. He would be helping other team members to get things done.

> This seems very important to you. Let's explore what options you have to get that change with Harry.

Dance continues

EXERCISE 6: CREATE YOUR OWN GAP QUESTIONS

What you will need: Pen, Reflection
How long it will take: 5 min
Dancing mindset: Be Curious, Be Specific

▶ Write out the Goal and Gap questions that you can apply in your conversations with an Octopus. Make the questions feel natural to your personal style. Writing them down will help you remember them when needed.

WRITE YOUR OWN GOAL AND GAP QUESTIONS

Goal Questions

Gap Questions

Tip: The Goal question can create inspiration for the Octopus as it lifts them from their current challenges.

Q. What if the Goal is just the opposite to what has happened?

A. Occasionally, the Goal could be as simple as the opposite to the problem the Octopus has described. However, because you have Pivoted (Moment 1) to what the person wants, it will usually be different from what they originally were thinking.

Q. What if I get a broad Goal rather than a specific, targeted Goal?

A. This is the most common mistake: the goal the Octopus expresses is too broad or generic. This means it is unlikely to be clear enough to motivate the Octopus to strive for it. Help them break their bigger goal down into small parts. The more you can help the Octopus to articulate a more specific and targeted goal, the more they will be able think of new ways to achieve it as you progress the dance. This means that closing the Gap will be more worthwhile.

Q. What if they cannot think of the Goal?

A. You will need to help them. Examples of helpful questions are 'What is a small win you would want?' You can help them prioritize the Goal by asking 'What is the thing that matters most?' Then keep dancing.

Q. What happens if I miss the Gap?

A. If you miss the Gap, the dance has no leverage with the person when you get to the Edge moment. The Gap gives purpose and a reason to change. It is a motivator and driver. If you miss it, go back and re-do!

SUMMARY – WHEN TO USE THE GAP MOMENT

When the Octopus...

Is not clear about what they are trying to achieve.

Is not motivated to solve the issue.

Is not clear about the benefits of changing something.

Has talent that you want to develop.

Needs you, as their coach, to inspire new thinking.

DANCING MINDSET REQUIRED

◀💬 Be Specific: Why is the issue important to solve?

◀💬 Seek Mutual Value: How valuable is this issue when solved?

Write down when you can use a Gap moment

NOTES PAGE

MOMENT 3

THE EDGE

'We cannot solve our problems with the same thinking we used when we created them.'

Albert Einstein

The Edge moment is the question that challenges the thinking and solution provided by the Octopus. It is critically checking and comparing the proposed 'change' against what they have already done and what they want.

Definition of Edge: Incisive or penetrating quality; a favorable margin; keenness or intensity of desire or enjoyment.

WHY IS THE EDGE IMPORTANT?

Improves decision making

The Octopus is making the decision. You want the Octopus to make the decision. The word *decision* comes from '*de*' meaning 'away' and '*cision*' meaning 'cut'. Making a decision means they are effectively 'cutting away' other choices and taking one action. The Edge moment means the Octopus starts to narrow their focus on how their chosen course of action will actually work.

Fosters confidence

The Octopus often has the solution to their own problem in mind, and when they express why their idea is going to work, you are fostering their confidence. As their dance partner, you are bringing out their inner thoughts by asking the Edge question at the right moment. You are drawing out what the Octopus is thinking, so you need to be as non-judgemental as possible. To do this, make sure your body language is open and supportive and your tone is encouraging. This will ensure they continue to express why they think their chosen course of action will work better than what they are currently doing.

Changes the relationship

You are their dance partner/coach, not just a sounding board. You have an obligation to challenge what you see and hear. You will draw respect from your partners by the way you introduce 'Edge' into your conversation.

KEY ELEMENTS OF THE EDGE

Reality check

The Edge can be used to make the Octopus consider roadblocks and other factors that will impact their choice. You are asking them to give you a compelling explanation of how what they are proposing is going to work. It gives you the opportunity to observe the attitude and skills the Octopus uses to solve their challenges in the workplace.

Focus

Asking the Octopus to make the proposed solution detailed, targeted and specific is important to achieving the change the Octopus wants. As they respond to your questions, notice how the questions help them to focus on developing their proposed solution further, helping to make it clearer (not broader).

Timing

The Edge moment needs to happen at the halfway mark of the time you have set for the dance. It allows the Octopus time to start looking at options to close their Gap and achieve their Goal. The Octopus has the opportunity to further develop their selected choice while they are with you. Continue to dance with them after the Edge moment question to help the Octopus's decision become clearer.

Ownership

By creating the conditions for the Octopus to make the decision, you are increasing their sense of ownership and accountability. The articulation and clarification of their decision to you makes the action tangible. It is the psychology of 'I said it, therefore it becomes mine'. This is why 'asking and not telling' is central to any sustainable behaviour and performance change.

How to build an Edge moment

To build the Edge moment, you will need to connect your question back to what the Octopus has said at the Gap moment. Your role is to challenge whether that proposed solution will 'close the Gap'. To help you build your Edge questions:

▶ Refer back to what has been said earlier in the conversation.

▶ Find out what would be different from what they are doing now.

▶ Connect to the passion they may have shown earlier in the conversation about the issue.

The Octopus's proposed solution should be expressed in a way that shows they have energy and emotion to take action. The decision has to matter to them for real action to take place. Once you have asked the Edge question, keep dancing to make sure the Octopus has the clarity they need to act.

'Sometimes the moments that
challenge us the most, define us.'

Deena Kastor

The Edge questions

Examples of Edge questions:

How is what you have proposed different from what you have already tried?

How will this proposed approach close the gap?

What does your choice mean to you?

If you do this <*insert decsion*>, what does it mean for you?

Why is what you are proposing going to work?

What happens if it does not work for you the first time?

Case Study Continues

Previous: Page 72

Next: Page 96

Dancing with Mike. Moment 3

Previous: Page 72

Next: Page 96

Update: The coach wants to find out what Mike thinks he can do to begin solving the real problem. Notice how the coach challenges Mike.

COACH

MIKE

> What do you propose to do about these issues to get your goal?

> I need to talk him through how his attitude is affecting us and let him know that I am on the same side.

MOMENT 3: The Edge. Challenge the option or solution.

> How is that different to what you have already tried?

> I have not tried to talk about being on his side and that I want his point of view.

> Tell me about getting his point of view.

> He doesn't think I know what he is doing.

> What else?

> I don't think he trusts me. I think he believes I have more resources which I should be freeing up to help him.

> Why is trust a different way of thinking about the issue?

> He only mentioned resources once but I suspect the real issue is he does not trust my intentions.

> How does that change your approach?

> Significantly. I need to gain his trust to get what I want, not just try solve the immediate issue we have.

> Building trust is important to get the change you want. How are you going to do that?

Dance continues

Reactions to the Edge moment

WATCH: The Octopus may notice the change in the tone of the dance. The Octopus's response to your Edge question should be energetic and engaged. You are challenging their decision and reasoning. Increased energy and excitement are good signs that your dance is working. Other reactions to look for are:

▶ Defensiveness: The Octopus may have thought they already had the best answer. See table below for responses.

▶ Big pauses: Don't be afraid of silence. It can help the Octopus to go further into their own thinking.

▶ Respect will grow: The Octopus will see you as an equal who wants to get the best from them.

EXAMPLES OF HOW TO ASK A FOLLOW-UP QUESTION TO THEIR REACTION.

'There is only one way.'	> 'How do you know that is true?'
'I cannot think of another way.'	> 'Let's go back to the gap.'
'I don't know. What do you think?'	> 'I am interested in your thoughts.'
'Can I come back to you?'	> 'Sure. What will you think about?'

Case Study Continues

Previous: Page 74

Next: Page 98

Dancing with Sarah. Moment 3

Update: The coach wants to see what options Sarah has for changing Harry's behaviour.

COACH

SARAH

So what can you do with Harry to help him be accountable?

I need to work through his workload and milestones.

Sounds like you're figuring out the issues. What else could you try?

I could make him aware of the impact on me?

What would be the benefit of doing that?

Well, he would understand how it is making my job harder and the reason I am being tougher on him.

MOMENT 3: The Edge. Challenge the option or solution.

So are you doing this for him or for yourself?

That second option is more for me, which is not going to help.

You would feel better though!

I would. (smiling)

What could you do if you wanted to inspire Harry rather than make him feel guilty?

Applying the Power of 3 Plus here helps to increase alternative options.

Inspire! That's a big stretch. I am a bit stuck... What do you think I should do differently?

MOMENT 3: The Edge. Challenge the option or solution.

I want to see what you can come up with.

Dance continues

EXERCISE 7: CREATE YOUR OWN EDGE QUESTIONS

What you will need:	Pen, Reflection
How long it will take:	5 min
Dancing mindset:	Be Curious, Be Specific, Be Aligned

▶ Write out the Edge questions that you can apply in your conversations with an Octopus. Make the questions feel natural to your personal style. Writing will help you remember them when needed.

WRITE YOUR OWN EDGE QUESTIONS

Remember: This is making the Octopus think about the action they are proposing. Make sure your questions are open and linked to what they have said.

Q. What if they get defensive?

A. Remember, this is a Dance. Keep your tone supportive and play back what they have said in the Pivot and Gap moments.

Q. What if the option/solution is similar to what they tried before?

A. Call it! Let the Octopus know that their chosen action sounds like what they have done before. You should reflect on whether your Gap or Pivot moment questions were explained or explored enough.

Q. What if they don't agree that they said something earlier?

A. Remember, take notes! Without notes, you will not have the detail to play back what was said with confidence. The reason they may have forgotten is their thoughts are tangled. Remind them and get them to clarify what they meant earlier.

SUMMARY – WHEN TO USE THE EDGE MOMENT

When you, as the coach...

Want to shift the way someone is thinking.

Have a low performer you want to challenge.

Have a high performer who can be inspired.

Want the person to reflect on what they have been saying.

Want them to take ownership of the solution.

Want the person to see a blind spot in their performance.

DANCING MINDSET REQUIRED

Bring Energy: This part of the dance should be challenging.

Be Curious: How do they think their decision will work?

Write down where you can use the Edge moment

NOTES PAGE

MOMENT 4
THE CONVERTOR

'Oh I'm sorry, I didn't realise that you're an expert on my job and how I should do it. Please continue while I take notes'

Internet site: Your Cards (Present day)

The Convertor moment is used to keep you and your partner dancing. When you feel the urge to tell or share your own ideas, convert that advice into a question. This moment is how you keep the Octopus thinking and developing their solution while harnessing your experience.

Definition of Convert: To change or cause to change in function or character.

THE CONVERTOR

DANGER MOMENT: KEEP THE DANCING MINDSET

This is the time in the dance when you are most likely to stop coaching. The temptation is to begin telling the Octopus what they should do because you think you have the better option. By offering, suggesting or telling them the answer to an issue, you remove accountability, ownership, empowerment, and confidence, stifle innovation and let the Octopus off the dance floor.

> KEEP THE DANCING MINDSET AND LEARN
> HOW TO CONVERT YOUR CONCERNS.

IMPORTANT THINGS TO KNOW ABOUT THE CONVERTOR

Your experience can help when you share it well

You have the experience that can help to open up the Octopus to new thinking or a better choice. The key is to convert that experience into a question. In simple terms, it is changing a statement (your concern) into a question. By asking them a Convertor question, you are opening them up to thinking in a new direction about things they may not have considered. They are learning how to think about solving their issue without being taught or told.

Asking questions is tougher than telling

Don't compromise. Asking questions is not weak! Just make your questions well constructed to get the best responses. You have the right as the dance partner to make sure that a quality outcome is achieved. Keep dancing even when telling seems easier.

It's about the Octopus, not the problem

Since the Pivot moment, you have been focused on the Octopus not the problem. Keep your Convertor moment questions focused on the person. This is as simple as including 'you' in the Convertor moment question. For example, 'How will you manage the competing priorities?'

KEY ELEMENTS OF THE CONVERTOR

Convert if the ideas to solve the issue have stalled

The risk for new coaches is to continue asking questions (dancing) that do not advance the Octopus's thinking. When you want more specific thinking from the Octopus, apply the Convertor moment. You need to trust your judgment. If it feels like the dance has stalled – don't waste time. Use the Convertor moment when you want to progress the dance.

The Octopus learns from the question

The Convertor moment shows the Octopus the type of questions they should be asking themselves in the future.

The Octopus might be right (and you're not!)

A key benefit of using Convertor moment questions is that the Octopus might be right and may have already thought about everything you were concerned about. They may even have come up with an answer that you had not considered. That is why it is important to be neutral. By asking the Convertor question, you are checking that they have considered other factors. There is a good chance that they will come up with a better solution than you would have.

How to build a Convertor moment

▶ List the fears, risks or concerns that you have and convert them into neutral questions.

▶ You create a neutral question by placing a 'what' at the front of your concern or advice.

My Concerns

I think it will cost a lot.

I worry about the other priorities.

There are other stakeholders to consider.

They are not considering the strategy.

I am not sure of the value.

I want to make sure they have considered safety.

My Experience

We have policies that cover this.

This has been tried before.

There is a project team working on this same issue.

Keep the Dancing Mindset

This is the time and place in a conversation that most needs you to keep the Dancing mindset. You want to keep dancing with the Octopus but you want to move the conversation forward. This is a great time to start to increase the quality of the Octopus's options by using your knowledge and experience in the right way; this is the way to do it.

The Convertor questions

What is the cost of this option?

What about your other priorities?

Who else will this affect?

How do you see this supporting our strategy?

How would you measure this?

What safety issues would you need to consider?

What current policies that cover this?

Where has this been tried before?

How can the project team help with this issue?

The tone of the questions needs to be kept neutral. Keep the Dancing Mindset as curious, not demanding. Your tone determines how your words will be interpreted.

Case Study Continues

Previous: Page 84

Next: Page: 110

Dancing with Mike. Moment 4

Update: Mike now knows he needs to build trust, but notice that the coach has to open Mike up to other ideas.

COACH

MIKE

Building Trust is important to get the change you want. How are you going to do that?

> I think I will take him out for a coffee and a chat.

What makes you think that will work?

> I can get to know him in an informal way, and then we can talk about his issues.

 MOMENT 4: Convert your concern about the informal coffee meeting

If one of the issues is that he is under time pressure, how do you think he will interpret a 'coffee ' catch up.

> He is under pressure so the coffee idea might just be more evidence of me not understanding him.

So what is another way to change the dynamic with him?

> I need to talk with him before the operational meeting next week. I should set up a pre-meeting.

What are the important things for you to ask in that meeting?

> I need to find out about his workload?

What else do you need to know?

> I'm not sure what you mean.

 MOMENT 4: Convert your experience about the content meeting.

How are you going to get him to open up about how he views you and your team?

> That is a tougher conversation; however, if I am going to improve the relationship, we need to talk about these perspectives.

Dance continues

Reactions to the Convertor moment

WATCH: If you get the tone right, the Octopus will start to show how they think and what process they have gone through to reach their solution.

Here are some of the reactions you may get from the Convertor moment question.

▶ Reflective silence: If they do not have an answer to the question that you asked, they may need more time to think of their response. Give them time to think it over, then keep dancing.

▶ More energy. You are pushing along their thinking but not telling them what to do. The Octopus starts to realise you are not going to give the answer, so they will start to appreciate that they need to do more thinking if they are responsible for solving the issue.

▶ Increase in collaboration: The Octopus starts to think through in more detail what they are going to do. This increased focus on getting them to respond to your questions will develop their capability as they start to see the value of talking (dancing) with you.

KEY TIP : MAKE THE CONVERTOR QUESTION - OPEN!

Open questions encourage dancing as the Octopus cannot just say yes or no.

Open questions usually start with 'What', 'How', 'Why', 'When'.

Closed questions start with 'Have', 'Could', 'Would', 'Should', 'Do'.

Case Study Continues

Previous: Page 86

Next: Page: 112

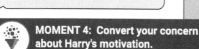

Dancing with Sarah. Moment 4

Update: Sarah is stuck. She cannot think of a way of talking to Harry. The coach can help by using the Converter moment.

COACH

SARAH

> I hear you're wanting to try something different. What do you think motivates Harry?

>> He likes recognition for doing good work.

 MOMENT 4: Convert your concern about Harry's motivation.

> How do you know that?

>> I am not 100% sure, but he seemed to respond to public acknowledgment of his work.

> What is the problem with not knowing for sure?

>> You're right. I am guessing. Harry has been doing the role for a while. I should know more about his aspirations.

> What are his aspirations?

>> Harry applied for my job when it was vacant. When I got it, I talked with him, but I have not followed that up with him since then.

> That sounds important. What conversation could you have with him to motivate him rather than manage him more?

>> I should have seen this earlier. I need to start a conversation about his role and aspirations.

 MOMENT 4: Convert your experience about getting a behaviour change.

> How can you do that and still work on the accountability issue?

>> I am sure that if I can link his current work to help him achieve his future goals, then he will get back to his best performance. I've missed that link between those things.

> You have an approach for Harry. How can you apply this to others in your team?

>> I need to find the motivators for each person. I have been so busy, but it is critical.

Dance continues

EXERCISE 8: DO NOT ANSWER A QUESTION

What you will need:	Timer
How long it will take:	1 hour
Dancing mindset:	Be Curious, Bring energy

Choose an hour of your day when you will answer every question you are asked with a question. The aim is to practice not answering a question. Some other guidelines are as follows:

▶ You can only give your opinion or advice as an open question. Take your time to make sure that your response reflects what you want the person to think.

▶ Tip: Keep your tone interested but neutral.

REFLECT: WHAT REACTION DID YOU GET?

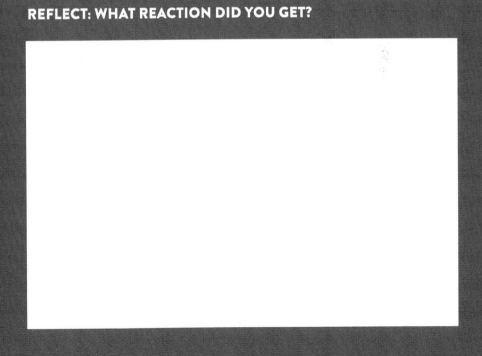

EXERCISE 9: CREATE YOUR OWN CONVERTOR QUESTIONS

What you will need:	Pen, Reflection
How long it will take:	5 min
Dancing mindset:	Be Curious, Seek Mutual Value, Be time-bound

Make a note of concerns you are likely to have with your Octopus and then convert them into questions to keep the Octopus thinking and responsible.

Issues or concerns I have	**Converted to a question**
....	....
....	....
....	....
....	....
....	....

NOTES PAGE

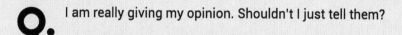
Q. I am really giving my opinion. Shouldn't I just tell them?

A. This is a common feeling for inexperienced dancers. You need to keep the Dancing Mindset and be aware the reason for asking not telling. Don't take over. It ruins the dance.

Q. What if they have not considered my concern? What happens next?

A. You have elevated and expanded the Octopus's thinking. Now ask them to take the new thinking and reconsider their options. Keep dancing for the new proposed option to get the Octopus to work out the choice. Invest time in this part of the conversation. The Octopus can come back to you later after thinking the option through in more detail. This is a very good way to save and make the dance effective.

Q. What if I feel like the Octopus has chosen an option that is not going to work?

A. The challenge is for you, as the coach, to turn that broad feeling into a number of specific converted questions. You can always go back and ask an Edge moment question, which could be as simple as 'Why do you think this will get the outcome you want?' If your questions are asked neutrally, you will be able to guide their thinking rather than stop it.

SUMMARY – WHEN TO USE THE CONVERTOR MOMENT

You have the answer and want to help them.

Your experience is telling you there is something they are missing.

You want them to consider additional things outside their role.

You know something they don't that will impact their choice.

You want to still coach but want also to progress the conversation.

Note: This moment is really to help you as the coach. Only use this moment if you think of a concern that may not have been considered.

DANCING MINDSET REQUIRED

Seek Mutual Value: I am able to share my experience.

Be Curious: What have they considered in the solution?

Write down where you can use the Convertor moment

NOTES PAGE

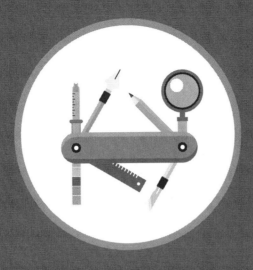

MOMENT 5

ABLE 2.0*

'Just because I say I will and I want to do it, doesn't mean I can'

Ben Larkey

Able 2.0 is the moment you are moving the Octopus from thinking to doing. It gets them to take the first step to solving their challenge.

THIS IS A GAME CHANGER

* 'Able' is short for 'Cap-able' of doing what they said. The '2.0' means an improved second version, better than the '1.0' version.

WHY THE ABLE 2.0 IS CRITICAL

The dance does not finish when the Octopus says what they are going to do

Just because the Octopus has reached awareness and says they are going to do something does not mean that they can. When the Octopus goes back to their environment, they often find it difficult to implement what they want to do. That means you want the Octopus to know whether they can actually do what they say they will do after the dance. You will need to get them to practice their first step with you. For example, if they said they will give feedback to a colleague, then you get them to role play the first few sentences with you. You are making their intention become more concrete and real. You will see if they are able to take the first step. Keep dancing till the Octopus feels capable of taking the first step of their planned action.

The Octopus needs to take the first step with you

There can be a skills gap in the Octopus's ability to do what they need to do. They might not know about this gap until they start to carry out the chosen action. When they role play with you, the Octopus gets to experience the 'skills-gap' in their capability much earlier. This is a powerful opportunity to help them with a micro-skill that will help them to put into action what they want to do. As the coach, you get to see if the dancing and critical moments have prepared the Octopus for this moment. If the Octopus is motivated to practice their action with you, the previous moments have worked. If the Octopus does not want to practice, you need to go back and find out what is really stopping them from solving their issue.

The Octopus will feel the switch to doing rather than talking about their problem. This change will be reflected in the language they use with you. The Octopus will start using words such as 'I' or 'me' rather than 'they' or 'you'. A sense of ownership is achieved.

KEY ELEMENTS OF ABLE 2.0

Moving from thinking to doing

The Able 2.0 question is about getting the Octopus to focus on doing what they said they would do. Up to this point in the dance, the Octopus has become clearer in their own mind about the issue, what they can do to close the gap and what is different. All that current thinking means that at this stage, the next steps are conceptual and theoretical. You can get them to translate their thoughts into practice by experiencing the first steps with you.

Ready and willing, but not Able

Missing this moment is one of the major reasons that coaching fails in the real world. The Octopus wants to act, but when faced with 'doing' it, hesitates, procrastinates and does not act. And if the Octopus does act and fails, they are likely to have a poor experience while trying to implement their new behaviour. This may cause them to lose confidence, and their performance will be affected. By practicing the chosen option, the quality is likely to be higher because it has been rehearsed.

Saves time and builds talent

You will help the Octopus save time and effort because they will not have to go back to their workplace and think about how to implement their option. They have already had a practice run with you. Every minute you invest now in getting the Octopus to role play or practice with you, will save you rework later. You are closing the last reason for the Octopus to not take action.

How to build an Able 2.0 moment

▶ Use key words: 'Show me' or 'Walk me through...'

▶ Connect to their motivation: 'You have said this will matter....' or 'Let me see you how your solution will work...'

▶ Confirm the importance of solving this issue: 'This is important to you ...' or 'The first step is...'

Examples of Able 2.0 responses to the Octopus's stated solutions

Octopus: Make a phone call...
Action: Role play the call with them.

Octopus: Write an email...
Action: Watch them draft the first sentences.

Octopus: Have a meeting...
Action: Role play how they would start it.

Octopus: Give feedback...
Action: Role play the start with me.

Octopus: Better manage my diary...
Action: Get your diary and show me.

Have confidence. Ask the Able 2.0
question, then participate in the practice
session with the Octopus.

Definition of Able 2.0

Able is short for 'Cap-able' of doing what they said. It also means that you are developing the capability of the Octopus.

2.0 means a improved version. The first version is called 1.0. When this is updated with a better and improved version it is called version 2.0

Examples of Able 2.0 showing the first step after dancing. Here are some example sentence starters:

What is your first step?

Role play with me how you will...

Show me how you are going to do that.

Walk me through your approach.

Show me how you will apply your new skills.

Practice with me how you will say that.

Why this is a game changer!

This final Able 2.0 moment completes the dance because they are 'doing' what they have just been 'thinking'. It means every dance with an Octopus will have a concrete, specific experience at the end to ensure what was said can be done.

Case Study Continues

Previous: Page 96

Dancing with Mike. Moment 5

Update: Mike sees the benefit of the new conversation; however, the coach wants to make sure he can do it.

COACH　　　　　　　　　　　　　　　　　　　　　**MIKE**

> When are you going to have the conversation?

> The operational meeting is next week. I will set up a pre-meeting with him today.

> What are you going to say to get him to come to that pre-meeting with you?

> I will send a meeting request.

> I mean what are you going to say so that he wants to come to that pre-meeting with an open mind?

> That is hard to put it in writing...I will have to call him

> **MOMENT 5: Practice the approach for the call.**
>
> [Pause]. Try that call with me.

> OK. I might get this wrong!

> It's just a practice run.

> Here goes. 'Hi, Sam. It's Mike.'

Coach role playing being Sam

> 'Hi, Mike. What can I do for you?'

> 'Actually, it's more what I can do for you.'

> 'That's interesting.'

> 'Seriously. I know things have been really busy for you and your team, and I wanted to meet before the Operations meeting to figure out a way for me to be of better support to you.'

> 'I would like that. How about over coffee?'

> 'I would like that. I will email through the meeting details.'

> What did you think of the practice run?

> Thanks. Practicing really made it clear to me. I will keep you updated.

Dance completed

Reactions to the Able 2.0 moment

WATCH: Most Octopuses think they can do what they just agreed to do. However, when they are asked to show you, the Octopus discovers whether they really can!

Here are some of the reactions you may get from the Able 2.0 moment.

▶ Surprise: They think that the dance has finished, and they were about to leave.

▶ Uncomfortable: They have said they are going to do it but then struggle to actually do it, which feels awkward.

▶ Avoidance: 'Let me come back to you.' Don't let them do that. What you are seeing is the REAL reaction, and you can 'catch' any resistance or roadblocks that are stopping them. You can then choose to start another dance on that particular issue.

The action becomes real for the Octopus!

KEY TIP: THE ABLE 2.0 MOMENT IS ON-THE-JOB PRACTICE

You are getting them to practice with you. This replaces the need for training.

If you are doing a role play with the Octopus, set up the situation and roles being played. Always make the practice 'easy'. If you make it difficult, you risk losing the momentum you have gained from the dancing you have done.

Give them a minute to prepare. It helps them transition from thinking to doing.

Case Study Continues

Previous: Page 102

Dancing with Sarah. Moment 5

Update: Sarah has had a breakthrough with her thinking. She knows what she wants to do. The coach will help make sure it is done with skill.

COACH

SARAH

When can you talk to Harry about this?

> I am seeing him tomorrow at our weekly catch-up meeting.

How are you going to manage the conversation?

> I will bring up the topic of his future and then ask him to tell me what he is thinking.

You sound pretty clear.

> I am. This is important.

 MOMENT 5: Practice the approach for the meeting.

Before we finish, role play with me the first couple of minutes of the conversation with Harry.

> Here goes. 'Harry, I noticed your work has dropped off and I was thinking it could be because of concerns about your role and where you are going.'

What do you think about that approach?

> Not that good. It sounded very direct and almost blaming.

(Chuckle) It did. So what could you change?

> (Pause) Can I write this down?

Absolutely. That's a good way to prepare.

> Let's try that again. 'Harry, I realise I have been very task focused of late. I wanted to check in with you and see how things are going.'

Coach role playing being Harry

'Thanks for asking. I am finding things tough at the moment.'

> 'What is happening to cause that?'

'I find the new structure confusing, and I'm not sure where I can contribute. It not an excuse but I am not sure where I fit.'

> 'Let's work it out together. Where do you see yourself wanting to fit?'

How did the second approach go?

> Much better. I am actually looking forward to having the conversation.

I look forward to hearing how it goes and what you learn.

Dance completed

EXERCISE 10: CREATE YOUR OWN ABLE 2.0 QUESTIONS

What you will need:	Pen, Reflection	
How long it will take:	5 min	
Dancing mindset:	Bring energy, Be Time-bound	

▶ Write out the possible Octopus solutions that you are likely to experience at your work (e.g. Octopus says 'I will call and clear this up'), then write your Able 2.0 question that you can apply in your conversations with an Octopus.

WRITE YOUR OWN ABLE 2.0 QUESTIONS

Possible Octopus action	Converted to Able 2.0

Tip: Be inventive with your approach to this moment. The key is to take what they want to do and get them to practice the first step with you.

Q. What if they cannot show you or start the option they came up with?

A. It is great to know now what is holding them back! Take them back to the Gap or the Pivot moment to check if something was missed. Go back to their options and get them to choose a better solution. Apply the Edge moment to whatever they come up with next.

Q. What if they realise they do not have the skill to do what they need to do?

A. Well done. You have found that out before it has drifted or taken more time later. This is your call as a coach/leader. You can now do an 'on-the-job' skills session with them. If you have done this well, then the Octopus will be grateful for the skills to help them solve their immediate need. You can also develop a more formal training session with them later.

Q. How do I do the practice without being patronising? They said they will do it and now I am checking on them!

A. The key is to make the practice with you safe and simple. If the Octopus needs to prepare, give them a chance to get their thoughts in order. Keep the tone of the practice meaningful and realistic. After the first time you apply this moment with an Octopus, they will start to expect it.

SUMMARY – WHEN TO USE THE ABLE 2.0 MOMENT

You want to make sure they do what they said they would.

You have 'talked' about this before but nothing happened.

You see see that the person is unsure or hesitant.

You want to see the first step of the person's action.

You want to shorten the gap between 'thinking' and 'doing'.

DANCING MINDSET REQUIRED

Be Specific: The details matter for what you are going to do.

Seek Mutual Value: We are both benefiting from the conversation.

Write down where you can use the Able 2.0 moment

NOTES PAGE

DANCE MASTER CLASS

POWER OF
3 PLUS

'When you talk, you are only repeating what you
already know. But if you listen you may learn
something new.'

Dalai Lama

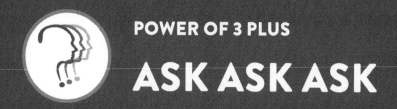
WHY DO WE ASK QUESTIONS?

Before an Octopus will decide to take a new action, they must be clear on what to do and and how to do it. Questions help the Octopus to express their issue and get clarity on what they want and how they can achieve it. Helping the Octopus to express what they think and feel is done by asking a flow of linked questions. A flow of linked questions requires the Octopus to 'go into themselves' to construct a response. This inward thinking can happen quickly. By continuing to ask questions, you are giving them the opportunity to untangle the components of their issues. Untangled thinking is required for the Octopus to make that decision to act and to own the next steps. Your flow of questions is the music of the coaching dance.

The flow of questions is the music of the dance.

One question is not a dance. The dance is made up of a series of linked questions that connect and build on what has been said. The answers are the guide to the next step. You stay focused on listening and responding to the answers your Octopus gives. The critical coaching moments are specific steps (questions) that you insert into the conversational dance to help your Octopus reach the most effective outcome.

Each of the Critical Coaching Moments is the first question of a Power of 3 plus sequence

Each of the moments is a point in the dance where you, the coach, change the tempo and direction of the conversation. By applying the Power of 3 Plus sequence at each of these moments, you are achieving your goal of helping the Octopus to become clear and act.

Barrier to the Power of 3 Plus

The two biggest barriers to the Power of 3 Plus are:

▶ Missing a Dancing Mindset

▶ Lacking one or two moments to help the conversation progress

EXPLAINED: POWER OF 3 PLUS

LISTEN using Ask, Ask, Ask (Power of 3 Plus)

The Power of 3 Plus looks like a questioning technique but is all about listening. Listening is critical, as the questions you ask have to come from the response to your previous question. Each question will follow from some part of the answer before it. You need to ask at least three linked sequential questions to get past the superficial responses and get to specific, unique and meaningful thinking. This flow of linked questions is how you create the music of the dance.

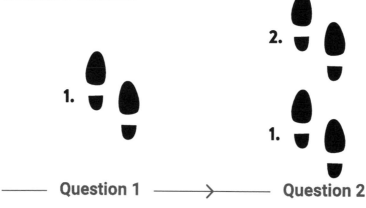

——— **Question 1** ———→

Start dancing.

Your first question is important; it starts the dancing/coaching. You are getting the person to start thinking.

Example: What happened?

Listen for what the Octopus says in response. You will be using the response to this first question to choose the next question.

Tip: Each of the five critical coaching moments has a starting question to propel you in a new and effective direction with your Octopus.

——— **Question 2** ———→

Keep dancing with the second question.

Question two comes from the response to question one. Listen for a key word or phrase that you can ask them to explain to you.

Example: What do you mean when you say <insert key word>?

Use the key words from the answer to choose the next question.

Tip: Most people stop asking after the second question. They miss the opportunity to find out more about what the Octopus was saying. Keep following what they say.

The follow-up questions help the Octopus to clarify their thoughts.

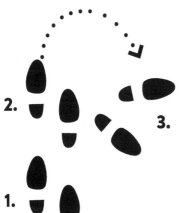

2.

3.

1.

Examples of 3 Plus questions to help you create your flow of questions.

What do you mean by the word <insert their word>?

Tell me more.

Can you give me an example?

How come?

Why is that?

What makes you say that?

What else does <insert their word> mean?

→ ———— **Question 3** ————→ ——— **'Plus' questions** ——→

Continue to dance with the third question.

Question three comes from the response to question two. Listen for a key word, phrase or feeling and ask the Octopus to expand on the point you have identified as important.

Example: You said <insert key word> give me an example? or How does <insert key word> affect you?

Use the key words from the answer to choose the next question. You will also start to notice that feelings start to appear in the conversation. Use any observed feeling to guide your next question.

REMEMBER: Every Octopus is unique once you flow to the third level of questions. You are now ready to move into the Plus questions.

The Plus questions happen after getting past the third level of asking. You have used the Octopus's own words to get them to express in detail what they are thinking.

Helping them to be specific allows the Octopus to clarify their thoughts.

The Octopus is now more engaged and thinking about their answers rather than your questions. Their responses will become more personal and reflective. Your dancing / coaching has started.

EXERCISE 11: THE THREE MINUTE POWER OF 3 PLUS CHALLENGE

What you will need:	Pen and paper
How long it will take:	3 min
Dancing mindset:	Be Curious, Aligned, Time-bound

Choose an Octopus that you know has an issue they need to work on. The intention is for you to stay focused on what they are saying but at no stage give your opinion.

Before you start the conversation:

▶ Set a timer on your watch or phone for three minutes

▶ Concentrate on open questions. Questions that start with 'What' and 'How' are open questions. Closed questions start with 'Did', 'Have', 'Do', and 'Can'. Closed question are not useful in dancing.

▶ Maintain positive body language, e.g. lean forward, smile, maintain open posture

Start the dance with the question: *What are your top two challenges?'*

▶ *Remember, no matter what happens, don't give your opinion or advice for three minutes.*

Reflection: What responses did you get from the Octopus?

What was different from your usual technique or process of asking questions?

Write that Down: Taking notes helps you to dance

Taking notes is important for capturing key words used by the Octopus that will help you to ask the next question. The Power of 3 Plus is about tracking the flow of the Octopus's thoughts and note-taking is the tool that helps you to do that. You do not need to write down every word used by the Octopus; however write the key words or phrases that you can use later. The Octopus will feel the dance has real depth and is important when they observe you taking notes.

▶ Taking notes helps you to concentrate on what the Octopus is saying.

▶ The act of writing means you can pick up on key words which allow you to make the conversation specific.

▶ You can easily connect and link different things that the Octopus says over the course of the dance.

▶ The act of writing signals that this is an important conversation and that what they say matters.

▶ Written notes provide a record that you can build on in your next dance.

▶ A template guide is provided on page 135.

TIPS FOR APPLYING THE POWER OF 3 PLUS

Watch that you do not stare at your page. Look up when you can, and look at your page only briefly while you are writing.

List the key words the Octopus uses and key points they make. Then put an old-fashioned <return key> arrow to show that the question comes from one of the points or words previously used.

Put your pen down and pay close attention if the Octopus gets emotional or shares a secret perspective. This helps the Octopus feel safe. When the point has been explored, pick up the pen and choose a new flow of questions.

EXERCISE 12: POWER OF 3 PLUS PRACTICE

What you will need:	Pen and paper, Timer
How long it will take:	4 min
Dancing mindset:	Be curious, Be Specific

This is a skill practice of the Power of 3 Plus.

Choose a conversation you need to have with an Octopus. Ask a starting question. Your next question must use a word or phrase they used when answering your questions. The following options can help you:

▶ What do you mean by the word <insert their word>?

▶ Tell me more.

▶ Give me an example.

▶ How does <insert their word> relate to <insert their word>?

Tip: Take notes during the dance.
Keep your tone and body language interested and engaged.

WHAT REACTIONS DID YOU GET FROM OTHER PEOPLE?

SUMMARY – WHEN TO USE THE POWER OF 3 PLUS

You want to understand why the person is behaving in a certain way.

You want to understand how the person thinks about the issue.

You and the other person are in conflict on certain topics.

You are lacking confidence (questions place the focus on the other person).

You want to be seen as a coach and leader within your team.

You believe the other person has more potential than they realise.

DANCING MINDSET REQUIRED TO USE THE RULE OF 3 PLUS

Be Curious: What are they thinking?

Be Specific: What do they mean?

Be Aligned: Are we talking about the same thing?

Bring Energy: Are we engaged?

Be Time Bound : Are we focused?

Seek Mutual Value: Are you both getting value?

The Dancing Mindsets need
the skill of Power of 3 Plus

GREAT QUOTES
ABOUT LISTENING

Listening is an art that requires attention
over talent, spirit over ego, others over self.

Dean Jackson

You can ask 'why' all you want, but
it doesn't mean a thing if you're
not listening to the answer.

Anonymous

Most people do not listen with
the intent to understand; they
listen with the intent to reply.

Stephen R Covey

We have two ears and one tongue so that
we would listen more and talk less.

Diogenes

PUTTING IT ALL TOGETHER

WHEN TO USE EACH CRITICAL COACHING MOMENT

QUICK GUIDE: THE FIVE CRITICAL COACHING MOMENTS™

This guide shows which critical coaching moment to use based on the behaviour and responses you observe from the Octopus.

START DANCING... ASK, ASK, ASK
Apply the Dancing Mindset and the Power of 3 Plus skill.

THE PIVOT

Change the focus to the Person, not the Problem.

The person is blaming others. ☐

The person is focused on the task, not on their own approach to the task. ☐

The person needs self-awareness about the impact of their actions. ☐

The person should be able to solve the problem but is not. ☐

The person has experienced the issue before. ☐

THE GAP

Identify and articulate the Gap between what is happening and what is wanted.

The person is not clear about what they are trying to achieve. ☐

The person is not motivated to solve their issues. ☐

The person is not clear on the benefit of changing something. ☐

The person has talent that you want to develop. ☐

You want to inspire new thinking. ☐

3 THE EDGE

Critically challenge the solution options against the reality, goal or gap.

You want to shift the way someone is thinking. ☐

You have a low performer you want to challenge. ☐

You have a high performer who can be inspired. ☐

You want the person to reflect on what they have been saying. ☐

You want the person to take ownership of the solution. ☐

4 THE CONVERTOR

Convert your concerns and experience into questions.

You have the answer and want to help them. ☐

Your experience is telling you there is something they are missing. ☐

You want them to consider additional things outside their role. ☐

You know something they don't that will impact their choice. ☐

You want to still coach but want to also progress the conversation. ☐

5 ABLE 2.0

Demonstrate they are able to do what they need to do next.

You want to make sure they do what they said they would. ☐

You have 'talked' about this before, but nothing happened. ☐

You see the person is unsure or hesitant. ☐

You want to see the first step of the person's action. ☐

You want to shorten the gap between 'thinking' and 'doing'. ☐

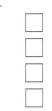

EXERCISE 13: WHICH MOMENTS DO I NEED?

What you will need:	Pen and paper. Refer to Exercise 1
How long it will take:	10 min
Dancing mindset:	Be Specific, Seek Mutual Value

▶ Intent: Recognise which moments will help you most when dancing with your Octopus. Often, you will need a combination of moments.

▶ Review the Octopus issues from Exercise 3 (page 38) and use the Quick Guide (page 126–127) to choose which of the Five Critical Coaching Moments would be the most useful to help 'untangle' your Octopus.

The Octopus issues that you are targeting.   **The Critical Coaching Moment for the issue that you are dealing with.**

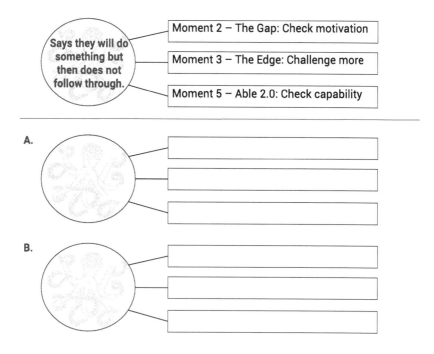

Says they will do something but then does not follow through.

Moment 2 – The Gap: Check motivation

Moment 3 – The Edge: Challenge more

Moment 5 – Able 2.0: Check capability

A.

B.

DANCING INTO REALITY

You now have all the skills and knowledge to be able to have a totally effective and productive conversation with anyone. You know and have practised the Rule of 3 Plus, which is the skill that keeps you in the asking mode. You know the Five Critical Coaching Moments are key questions that you apply at different times in the conversation to help the Octopus get clarity and ownership and take action.

The dancing mindset is the attitude that you bring to the conversation. Keep those dancing mindsets in your mind as you start to apply the skills and moments in the conversation. That dancing mindset will allow the skills that you have learnt to be applied and be successful.

Practical tips for your first dance

▶ Rule of 3 Plus is the skill that will make the biggest difference. Persist with your questions and use the linking aspect of the skill and you will see amazing results.

▶ Pick the Octopus and initiate the dance. Until asking is a habit and something that you do all the time, it is important to start every conversation consciously. Get your first question ready.

▶ Choose one or two Moments you want to use before you start. You don't need to use every moment in every conversation. By choosing just one or two moments, you will get comfortable with them. This will allow you to experience change and improvement and start to see the benefits of this approach.

▶ Tell the Octopus what you are doing. This may seem unusual; however, it can be really effective, especially if they're used to you giving an answer or they resist this new approach. Letting them know what you're doing makes them your partner in the dance and allows for some mistakes as you try the process.

▶ Keep an eye on time. Keep the dance moving and do not become stuck in one part of the dance. Trust the method, the Octopus and yourself.

EXERCISE 14: SUMMARISE THE FIVE CRITICAL COACHING MOMENTS ON ONE PAGE

What you will need:	Pen and paper. Review all your summary notes
How long it will take:	10 min
Dancing mindset:	Be Curious, Be Specific

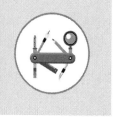

Transfer one question from each critical coaching moment onto this page.

 The Pivot

 The Gap

 The Edge

 The Convertor

 Able 2.0

 Power of 3 plus

Note: This summary page is an Able 2.0 moment for you. It is what you need to have to begin applying your new coaching method.

START DANCING!

YOUR FIRST FULL DANCE

GO BACK TO EXERCISE 3 - PAGE 38 (if you need to)

Intent: To prepare before you start your first dance with the Octopus.

▶ *Identify the Octopus* with whom you want to have a better relationship or whose performance you want to enhance. Write their name in the circle.

▶ *Identify the 'tentacle' issue or opportunity* you have observed. Use your notes from Exercise 3 to help you.

▶ *Remember,* this is only your perspective. Issues will become clearer as you find out more information from the Octopus.

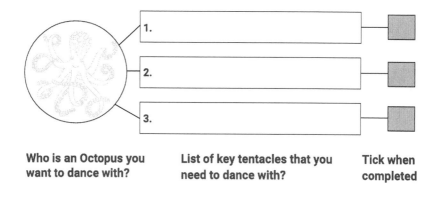

| Who is an Octopus you want to dance with? | List of key tentacles that you need to dance with? | Tick when completed |

CHECKLIST FOR DANCING:

☐ 5 Critical Coaching Moments Summary Sheet Ready

☐ Note Page Ready

☐ Timer / Watch Ready

☐ Dancing Mindset Ready

DANCING
NOTES PAGE

Write your notes in each moment as they happen in the conversation.

Octopus: _____   Topic _____

Time: ▽   What happened? _____
_____

○ | PIVOT

○ | GOAL   GAP

○ | EDGE   ▽ CONVERTOR

○ | ABLE

ACTION: Summary

EXERCISE 15: REFLECT ON YOUR REACTIONS TO THE FIRST DANCE

What you will need:	Pen and paper. Review all your summary notes
How long it will take:	5 min
Dancing mindset:	Be Curious, Be Specific

After applying the Five Critical Moments in a conversation, reflect on what you learned:

	Yes	No
I found out the reason for something happening.	☐	☐
I was able to stay on track (apply a couple of moments).	☐	☐
I consciously 'asked' versus 'telling' (mindset).	☐	☐
I held back on giving my opinion (convertor moment).	☐	☐
We both got mutual value (had moments).	☐	☐
They were more accountable for the next steps (Able 2.0).	☐	☐
I got the detail of what they think (Rule of 3 Plus).	☐	☐
I finished within the expected time frame (10 – 12 min).	☐	☐

WHAT IS THE MOST IMPORTANT NEW IDEA FOR YOU?

....

....

....

NOTES PAGE

CONGRATULATIONS! YOU ARE NOW DANCING WITH AN OCTOPUS

You have the skill,
knowledge and mindset to

Stop Telling and Start Coaching

Enjoy every conversation
and moment that you
create, and lastly....

PART D

GUIDES AND SUPPORT MATERIALS

OVERVIEW
THE FIVE CRITICAL
COACHING MOMENTS

Each of the the five moments are designed to impact the conversation and achieve a specific response from your dance partner. Each moment serves a purpose.

1 **THE PIVOT.** Change the focus to the Person, not the Problem.

2 **THE GAP.** Identify and articulate the Gap between what is happening and what is wanted.

3 **THE EDGE.** Critically challenge the solution provided against the reality, goal or gap.

4 **THE CONVERTOR.** Convert any concerns and your experience into questions.

5 **ABLE 2.0.** Demonstrate they are able to do what they need to do next.

'Don't wait for the perfect moment.
Take the moment and make it perfect.'

Anonymous

SUMMARY – THE FIVE CRITICAL COACHING MOMENTS™ AND POWER OF 3 PLUS

In every conversation, there are five critical moments

Asking a specific critical question at the right moment changes the direction of the dance and helps the Octopus to see, own and do their solution.

The Power of 3 plus

1. The Pivot Moment
2. The Gap Moment
3. The Edge Moment
4. The Convertor Moment
5. Able 2.0 Moment

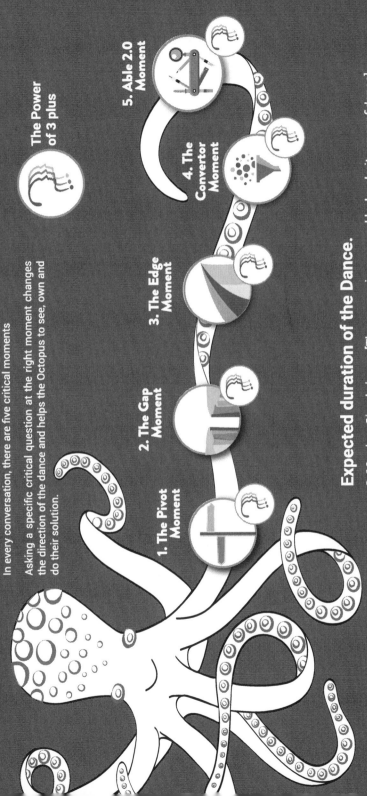

Expected duration of the Dance.

8-10 min = Simple issue [The person is open and lacks clarity or confidence]

18-20 min = Complex issue [The person is closed, defensive or has many relating issues]

LIBRARY OF MOMENTS

 The Pivot Moment

What do you think caused this?

What have you tried to do to influence this behaviour?

So why do you think they didn't understand?

What have you tried so far?

What have you done already to change this?

What impact is this having on you?

What would you do if this situation did not exist?

What happened to contribute to this?

What do you think led to this situation?

How have you reacted to this?

How does this issue make you feel?

What do you think your contribution has been in this happening?

How do you think you can get some change happening?

What do you think is driving this outcome?

What do you think you can do about this issue?

The Gap Moment

Part A: The Goal

What outcome are you looking for?

What does success look like?

How would you know if you got the change?

What would the change look like?

Part B: The Gap

How much difference is there between what is happening and what you want?

What do you see as the Gap between what you have versus what you want?

 ## The Edge Moment

How is what you have proposed different from what you have already tried?

How will you try to close the gap?

What does your choice mean to you?

If you do that, what does it mean for you?

Why is what you are proposing going to work?

What happens if it does not work for you the first time?

The Convertor Moment

Convert the Concern to a Question.

Cost: What is the financial impact?

Time: What is the time frame?

Workload: How does this affect your workload?

Other People: Who else will need to be considered?

Brand: How will you manage brand considerations?

Safety: What is the safety risk you need to manage?

Policy: What policy issues have you considered?

Quality: How will you maintain the quality with that approach?

 ## Able 2.0 Moment

What is your first step?

Role play with me how you will say that.

Show me how you are going to do that.

Walk me through your approach.

Show me how you will apply your new skills.

Practice with me. How you will say that?

DANCING TEMPLATE

Octopus: _____ Topic _____

Time: _____ What happened? _____
_____

PIVOT ( )

GOAL ( )   GAP

EDGE ( )   CONVERTOR

ABLE ( )

ACTION: Summary

MAPPING

G.R.O.W.*

TO THE FIVE CRITICAL COACHING MOMENTS.

*G.R.O.W. is a popular approach to guiding the process of coaching. It was made popular by John Whitmore, 'Coaching for Performance: Growing People, Performance and Purpose', 2002.

THE FIVE CRITICAL COACHING MOMENTS™ IN G.R.O.W.

The G.R.O.W. method of coaching is a great framework for coaches to use to guide their thinking. The Five Critical Coaching Moments™ can be mapped against each stage of the G.R.O.W. model to make it more impactful.

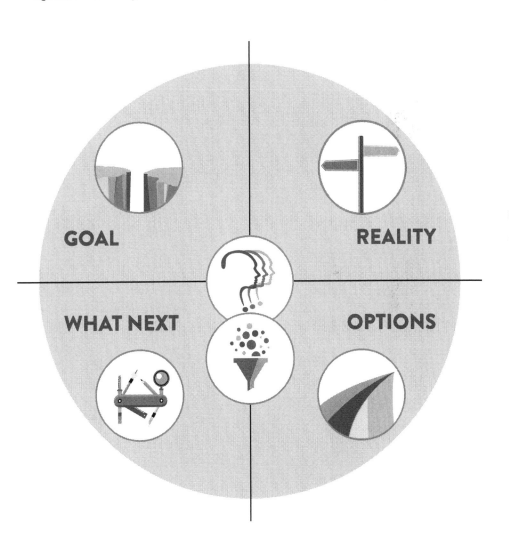

G.R.O.W. is a process.

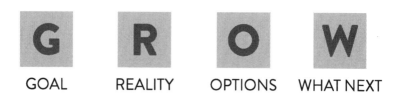

GOAL   REALITY   OPTIONS   WHAT NEXT

The ideal process flow for using G.R.O.W.

1. All conversations start in Reality, e.g. 'What happened?'

2. Use the Power of 3 Plus questioning in every section. Help the person to be specific and clear.

3. Reality: The 'Pivot Moment' should be used within the first 2 minutes of the conversation, e.g. 'What have you thought about so far?'

4. From Reality to Goal: To establish their goal(s), ask questions such as, 'What is the outcome you are after?"

5. Goal: The 'Gap Moment' occurs after establishing the Goal, e.g. 'What is the difference between your reality and goal?'

6. From Goal to Options: Explore options to achieve their goal, e.g. 'What options do you have?'

7. Options: The 'Edge Moment' is used to challenge their thinking, e.g. 'How is this closing the gap?'

8. Use the 'Convertor Moment' if you want to challenge the option, e.g. 'What costs must be considered?'

9. From Options go to 'What Next': Establish their plan going forward, e.g. 'What are you going to do? When?'

10. What Next: The 'Able 2.0 Moment' is used after they have committed to their first action step, e.g. 'Role play with me the first step you will take.'

NOTES PAGE

WOULD YOU LIKE BEN TO PRESENT A POWERFUL PROGRAM TO YOUR ORGANISATION OR ASSOCIATION?

Ben offers a unique approach to facilitating individuals and teams to articulate their personal drivers, needs and strengths, thereby enabling individuals to step up to the challenge of delivering on the aspirations of their business and creating a sense of energy in the way they work.

From professional associations and universities to global corporations and not-for-profit organisations, Ben's proven programs benefit people across all walks of life.

CHECK BEN'S WEBSITE

www.LearningRepublic.com.au

To request a speakers kit or for more information about Ben's speaking and workshop programs
Please contact:

Ben@LearningRepublic.com.au

Bulk purchase discounts available

Printed in Great Britain
by Amazon

84715195R00086